ALSO BY ALEXIS PAULINE GUMBS

*Survival Is a Promise: The Eternal Life of Audre Lorde*

*Undrowned: Black Feminist Lessons from Marine Mammals*

*Dub: Finding Ceremony*

*M Archive: After the End of the World*

*Spill: Scenes of Black Feminist Fugitivity*

primary

# primary

## after and with alma thomas

ALEXIS PAULINE GUMBS

Yale UNIVERSITY PRESS | NEW HAVEN & LONDON

Published with assistance from the Louis Stern Memorial Fund.



Yale University Press books may be purchased in quantity for educational, business, or promotional use. For information, please e-mail sales.press@yale.edu (U.S. office) or sales@yaleup.co.uk (U.K. office).

Set in Source Serif Pro type by IDS Infotech, Ltd.
Printed in the United States of America.

Library of Congress Control Number: 2026937603
ISBN 978-0-300-27930-6 (hardcover)

A catalogue record for this book is available from the British Library.

Authorized Representative in the EU: Easy Access System Europe, Mustamäe tee 50, 10621 Tallinn, Estonia, gpsr.requests@easproject.com

10 9 8 7 6 5 4 3 2 1

FSC
www.fsc.org
MIX
Paper | Supporting responsible forestry
FSC® C008955

for ariana, jared, and seneca

# contents

# primary

this is for the girl who studied oilslicks in parking lots looking for left behind rainbows. this is for broken beautiful black. this is why she studies even the wasteful portals. even the toxic sweat of fossils offers memory. this is for the girl who had no way to know what was beautiful.

she loved the wildness of her hair. she ate whatever made her smile. stubborn. she believed what nobody else could hear.

here.

this is for the girl who knew and acted. alive in every shade of purple.

for you sweetheart. refusing coloring book lines.
for all of us living between the notes of crayon boxes.
for each of you nurturing a taste for what the world tries to deny.

where daylight blurs, darkness calls.
where the child wonders, the empire falls.
knowing fails. creativity prevails.

in the cracks then, a color theorist is born.

*Winter Pool,* 1966. Watercolor and acrylic on paper, 30 × 22 ⅛ in. Sheldon Museum of Art, University of Nebraska–Lincoln, Olga N. Sheldon Acquisition Trust.

# first

Alma Woodsey Thomas, first graduate of Howard University in fine art, founder of the first art gallery for students in the public schools of Washington, DC, first Black woman to have a solo show at the Whitney Museum, and oldest sister of three girls, is best known today for her bright earth paintings of plants in motion. Stunning views of fields of flowers, as if someone who loves color is zooming by above. Born in 1891, before the invention of the airplane, she eventually made space paintings inspired by televised views of our solar system. Another view of the heavens.

When Alma was a child, before she and her family left the land of Georgia clay and mob rule[1] for the increased opportunities of Washington, DC, one of her younger sisters, Fannie, died of diphtheria, a disease of fluids transmitted through droplets holding bacteria. Today, diphtheria is rare in the United States because of vaccination, but when Alma Thomas was growing up, the transmission of these particular bacteria through a sneeze or a cough or from a surface could be deadly for a child. More deadly for Black children, whom a racist healthcare system routinely denied hospital care. When Fannie, a little girl named after her grandmother, died, the entire family must have been devastated. Maybe as the oldest sister, Alma felt she had been granted custody of Fannie's soul, an assignment to remember her well. A continuing connection. Grief also often moves through the release of fluid substances: tears, snot, the vapor of ragged breathing. Or maybe, if you are an artist, you create a ritual.

Maybe you would use earth to make a replica of your little sister in her Sunday best, bow in her hair, a knowing smile. Maybe you would shape the clay with your hands, glaze her carefully, and keep her beside you. Alma Thomas slept and dreamt next to a ceramic bust she made of her sister Fannie throughout her entire adult life. Maybe sister is a job that simply does not end with death.

When I think of Alma Thomas, who taught art for over thirty years at Shaw Junior High School, I think about the education Fannie did not live to receive. I think of the devoted teacher, working overtime, creating enrichment activities on weekends, working diligently on the Negro History Week committee, creating unprecedented art access in the DC public schools, providing guidance, care, and collaboration to children the age Fannie never reached.

When I think of Alma Thomas painting rushes of color, bright from the perspective of one flying above, I think not only of a woman whose life moved from what she called the "horse and buggy era" to the age of aerodynamics and into the space age, but also of a small angel's perspective.[2] What Alma would have wanted Fannie to see. In the most vivid of Alma Thomas's paintings I see Fannie's heaven, lovely with the care an older sister might offer a little girl who didn't get to grow up. Or maybe it was Fannie who taught Alma about perspective in her dreams.

I'm not saying that Alma Thomas's every painterly or pedagogical choice was made with Fannie in mind. Or that her status as an older sister and mentor to so many DC artists and Howard University students meant that "older sister" was a primary identity for Alma Thomas like it is for me. But if we center Fannie's eternal youth, instead of the dominant art market's tendency to center itself, we may learn something new about living, longing, and the generative pathways of sisterly love.

Once upon a time H. E. Mahal asked four Black artists, including Alma Thomas, for their "approaches to inhumanity." The idea was to see whether the work of Black artists could address in some way what the Scottish poet Robert Burns called "man's inhumanity to man." What survives is Alma's deflection of the terms of the interview: "Through color I have sought to focus on beauty and happiness rather than on man's inhumanity to man."[3]

She recentered her energy. Clarified her focus: beauty, happiness. The full interview has all but disappeared. But the quotation appears almost everywhere Thomas's work is displayed or discussed. Almost as if to give permission to a predominantly white set of viewers or institutions to enjoy her vibrant use of color without thinking about color's cruel calculus in a racist world. But what beauty? Whose happiness? The question of who the primary audience is for Thomas's work (including both the paintings as artifacts and the process of life as practice) could shed light on her primary aims.

Regenia A. Perry, one of the first African American women to attain a PhD in art history, did not include that ubiquitous quote in the profile on Thomas's work for her catalog *Free Within Ourselves: African American Artists in the Collection of the National Museum of American Art.* Perry, who was also the first African American person to serve as a guest curator at the Metropolitan Museum of Art, begins her section on Alma Thomas with a quote that includes these words: "Light is the mother of color. Light reveals to us the spirit and living soul of the world through colors."[4] The spirit and living soul already exist. And then comes the birth of color at the speed of sun. I am here for the revelation.

In 2022, noted lesbian feminist photographer Joan E. Biren mentioned that I should see the new Alma Thomas retrospective *Everything Is Beautiful* while it was on view at the Phillips Collection in Thomas's hometown of Washington, DC, but I missed it. When I learned that the exhibit was showing at the Frist Art Museum in Nashville, where I went a few months later to honor the retirement of crucial Black feminist theorist and teacher Hortense Spillers, I knew I couldn't miss it again. My partner and I would spend a morning there, I thought. But when I saw the scale of the paintings, the depth of the research, the philosophical wonder of Alma's view of the world, not to mention the replicas of her fabulous outfits and her brightly appointed living room, I knew that I would need to spend more time listening to what her work was teaching me. I couldn't stop wondering what it meant for a Black woman born in 1891 near Columbus, Georgia, at a time when color was used to enforce a deadly racial code, to become the greatest color theorist in the world. That wasn't the lesson of a morning, to mull over during lunch. It seems a lesson for many lifetimes. So I never left. I created a ritual.

I bought the catalog at the *Everything Is Beautiful* exhibit in Nashville, and then I went home and ordered all of the materials I could find by and about Alma Thomas, including a calendar. And then for the 365 days of a full calendar year I started every morning, first light, looking either at an image of an Alma Thomas painting, an archival photograph, a study, or a sketch. I am happy to share that Alma Thomas's archival papers, organized and preserved by her sister Maurice, are fully digitized and available on the website of the Smithsonian Archives of American

Art. Prompted by the paintings and these artifacts, every day I wrote poetry that startled and astounded me. It wasn't until I had written for a whole year that I finally read back over what I had been writing. I still don't know what it is. A partial index of my childhood associations with color? A testimony of the taste of being in love? A listening space for Alma to whisper her dreams into the present? A psychedelic record of a year where nothing made sense and yet life shone so brightly I wanted to remember it? And what if Alma Thomas's primary audience is a Black girl who did not make it? "Fannie" means "the free one." What are all the free versions of us left back in the dirt of our becoming? What can they teach us?

Even though I still don't know how to categorize what I wrote in my year of Alma Thomas, it is my job to orient you to this offering just as much as it is my job to remain free beyond my own categorization. I don't know what you will find here any more than I know what you will see in an abstract expressionist painting. I have organized it in a way that feels right to me, but you can read this in any order. This is what I might do if I had the honor of curating Alma's works and archival traces on gallery walls and freeing them from all structures at the same time. As if poems and paintings were windows that open. In here, they are.

Each section of this book is part of a ceremony. I have offered guideposts that signal where I am in my unfolding understanding of why Thomas's life and work continue to teach and transform me. The unfolding is not over, but it is time to invite you into the ceremony. Following Thomas, I am working with contrast and resonance. I am working with reference and departure. You will learn about Alma Thomas in this work, but this is not primarily a study of Alma Thomas, and this is not an explication of the value of Black abstraction and color theory. The primary purpose of this work is to exemplify a practice of intimate time travel, impressionistic memory, gratitude, wonder, and care. My prayer is that you will find new ways to wonder about yourself, new colors of possibility, but especially new or renewed questions about relation as revelation. About accountability and devotion across loss. About beauty as an ever-present choice. A method. Not a given. But given to us again and again.[5]

Throughout the work I experiment, like Thomas, with repetition. There are palindromes and pantoums and free verse poems and block poems and multiple rhyme schemes. You do not have to already know that you are a student of poetry or a student of painting to engage with this work, though I have listed the images I was viewing when I wrote each poem and invite you to view them too. My most important invitation to you is to do what Alma Thomas did with Black DC, and what I did with Alma Thomas's work: stay. Stay and notice what comes through. Notice where you travel, where you find yourself. When you close your eyes. Where you open.

# invocation

# leaves

behind you light
and through you light
and with you shadow
and with you sight

and through you light
and shape and sound
and with you sight
and sky and ground

and shape and sound
surround your hands
and sky and ground
and reddened land

surround your hands
and fill your head
and reddened land
you left instead

and fill your head
with shadowed sound
behind the light
that leaves the ground

Ida Jervis, *Alma Thomas Working in the Studio,* c. 1968. Gelatin silver print. Alma Thomas Papers, c. 1894–2001, Photographs, box 6, folder 18, page 15, Archives of American Art, Smithsonian Institution, Washington, DC.

# exactly

exactly where the sun kisses your cheek
your forehead
precisely where the light breaks
into your face

your forehead
broadest portal
into your face
what color are your bones?

broad portal
tell us of the inside
what color are your bones?
acrylic blood

tell us of the inside
through your window
acrylic blood
test for the seasons

through your window
precisely where light breaks
best for the seasons
exactly where the sun kisses your cheek

Ida Jervis, *Alma Thomas Working in the Studio,* c. 1968. Gelatin silver print. Alma Thomas Papers, c. 1894–2001, Photographs, box 6, folder 18, page 15, Archives of American Art, Smithsonian Institution, Washington, DC.

# kitchen studio

welcome this unidentified woman
round to your roundest table
make her a plate of rainbows
feed her paint

round to the nearest vitamin
your spectrum of nutrition
feed her paint
and see how long she stays

your spectacle of sweetness
your gorgeous every day
your feminine longing stays
on plate and paper

you're gorgeous every day
georgia built that way
of paper plates
imaginary planes

georgia born and raised
on a deep diet of color
your plain imagination
welcome here

Wasyl Szkodzinsky or Ron Tunison, *Alma Thomas and an Unidentified Woman in Thomas's Kitchen-Studio,* 1972/73. Gelatin silver print. Alma W. Thomas Papers, Columbus Museum, GA.

# besides

with you here
beside yourself
the light can mountain your face
canyon your eyes
forest your breathing

if you stand beside a painting
of your painting self
time splits

the west unravels
into what can fit in your purse
besides your gloves
if you love

yourself enough
to sit here waiting
to become
the work
of art

i know you are

you can go
far.

but you don't have to.

Unknown photographer, *Alma W. Thomas Visiting* Black Matri-Images: *A Retrospective Exhibit of Paintings by Laura Wheeler Waring and Paintings and Prints by Elizabeth Catlett, Lois Mailou Jones, Alma W. Thomas, Morgan State College Gallery of Art, Baltimore, Maryland (December 4, 1972–January 15, 1973).* Color photograph. Alma W. Thomas Papers, Columbus Museum, GA.

# mosaic

the mosaic falls together when the walls fall apart.
think montserrat. how an island shows its youth by erupting.

in your dreams the falling leaves are golden magma.
in your window a tree is an entire world.
in your hands everything falls out its proper name.
or in your mouth the name for everything is beauty.

and
somewhere james baldwin is saying that the wretched of the
  earth will break the cobblestones of empire.
somewhere george washington is wearing other people's teeth.
somewhere soldiers march bewildered in a confetti parade that
  brings back the explosions they survived.
somewhere in a wounded mountain a miner reads the ruby
  blood of the canary.
the sky in its component parts is not blue

your hands show their youth by creating
trees demonstrate their faith by letting go
your window feeds you the sky in panes
your mouth sings your sister's truest laughter
your dream requires universes of light

the mosaic's freedom comes from remembering walls
the island remembers its name. drowns.

*Light Blue Nursery*, 1968. Acrylic on canvas, 49 × 47 ⅞ in. Smithsonian American Art Museum, Washington, DC, Gift of the artist.

# easter

light paints your bed in preparation
sun signs the corner of your day
light sweeps your floor abundant
sky grounds you in memory

sun through the window
is somebody's birthday
sky wants to tell you
your name

and since you were born
this morning azalea
ancestors watch
from their frames

flower resurrection
a menopausal sunday
the ancient ones
sing through your hands

if jesus still bleeds
and the earth drinks forgiveness
roll the pillows off your comforter
and stand

Roland Freeman, *Alma Thomas's Bedroom,* c. 1973. Digital scan of a contact sheet. Collection of Roland Freeman.

# earth and space, sky and sea

this is what my niece taught me.

once upon a time, not too too long ago i wrote a short vignette about the reality of the horned narwhal whale and the myth of the unicorn. theft and lies and who benefits from denying our beauty and then selling it back to us broken. in the vignette i feature a moment of my tiny niece touching a puzzle i bought her of emily winfield martin's "dream narwhal painting," which features a little black girl with two afro puffs carried peacefully through an underwater landscape by a gray and spotted narwhal. "bonita bonita" my toddler niece had repeated while her baby sister crawled below the table listening.

on another day, much more recently, i had the idea that maybe my niece and i could write about narwhals and unicorns together, now that she was eight years old and a published author. i read her the vignette about her younger self and said, "think about it and let me know." she didn't need to think about it. "i already have the story," she said. and chanted it to me right there from the bathtub. i tried to keep up with the momentum of her clarity. kenzie's story, forthcoming in its entirety, is called "on land and on sea." on the surface it is about a powerful, peaceful, and generative alliance between the unicorns and the narwhals forged by their youngest leaders. but through a parenthetical disclosure by the author i learned that the story under the story is about two sisters. the youngest narwhal and the youngest unicorn find each other and play together and grow their skills and wisdom. they know they are related even though they live very different lives. they always have a way to communicate with each other even across planes of existence, like land and sea.

the youngest unicorn (the leader of the unicorns) and the youngest narwhal (the leader of the narwhals) have other names in the story, but kenzie let me know before continuing to recount their solidarity: "that's me and penny." the artist, even in her interspecies allegory, is an inclusive big sister. that is part of the responsibility of being first.

it is their practice of working together across contextual differences that allows the very different sisters to "earn their powers." and as with all relationships the inner worlds of sisters may not be immediately apparent to all, but as my niece's lesson becomes the context through which we see all things, she lets us know:

> And now if you see loads of sparkles and shimmers in the seas, you will know it is the leader of the narwhals speaking to the unicorns.
>
> And someday if you see fireworks so big they reach to the ocean, you will know the leader of the unicorns is speaking to the narwhals.

such is the visuality of sisters communicating to each other across unimaginable distances. bright enough to light up the whole ocean, big enough to fill the sky.

i think alma thomas knew something about the color of this. a visual representation of love across everything.

i am still learning.

this is what my nieces are teaching me.

like my niece mckenzie, i am always a big sister. my siblings are always a part of my story, whether i tell you their names or not. in fact, one of the major lessons i learned from my years of creating poetry from the place where alma thomas's life and work meet my own is that the primary work of being a sister has been an impetus for my creativity, my urge to imagine a world worthy of those coming immediately behind me. the ethics of "first" that Alma Thomas knew within familial and institutional contexts.

like my niece mckenzie, i am an older sister to living siblings who have been my playmates and antagonists, my responsibility and my inspiration. shared stewards of different memory angles on what it meant to grow up in our geographic, familial, racial, and ethnic situation.

like my niece mckenzie, i am an older sister to a younger sister named penelope. but unlike my niece penelope, my sister penelope was the second daughter never born. she would be forty-one now, the daughter that my parents named during their first pregnancy after i was born and grieved when they experienced a pregnancy loss. i have visual memories of that time, but they might be copied and pasted from another time. waiting in a parking lot. my mother crying in the car. logic says i would have been too young to remember. but mckenzie remembers people who died before she was born. she sees her great grandparents in dreams.

and so i study mckenzie, who shows me in more than one way what it means to be the older sister of penelope, a responsibility i still hold, and listen for.

the other day. not so many days ago, my niece penelope read my mother and me a missive out of her baby book, a letter my sister ariana wrote to her before she was born. "we already love you," my sister confessed. "it is a gift to be a little sister," she explained, "you will never be alone." and then she added, "but don't ever let anyone push you around, not even kenzie." by the time my sister wrote this note and chose the name penelope for her daughter, she had experienced pregnancy losses of her own. none of us except my sister and my brother-in-law knew penny's name until after she was born.

penny is a real child. her own person beyond the echo of her name. a boisterous, creative, gonna jump from the couch and tackle you, let me walk up your body to do a backflip while you hold my hands, tangible, specific irreplaceable person. kenzie sisters penny by playing with her or ignoring her, backing her up or disagreeing with her, complaining about her or protectively claiming to be the only qualified translator of "penny language." her sisterwork includes tears, snot, scratching, the passing on of outgrown clothes, the unauthorized cutting of penny's hair with safety scissors. it is tangible.

and my sisterwork with ariana, jared, and seneca has been tangible too. kicking ariana under the table at an inside joke. lifting jared on my feet so he can fly like superman. not dropping baby seneca when he spit up directly into my just-pressed hair. and it has been verbal. in the past through help on school applications and now through phone calls, the exchange of social media memes, book recommendations, and on and on. so shall it be for a very long time, i hope.

my sisterwork with my imagined sister penelope can only be an abstract expression.

alma thomas was a big sister, when she was painting, when she was teaching. she was an all-the-time tangible big sister to her younger sister maurice who she dressed up with in costumes made by their mother. who she lived with throughout most of her adult life in the rooms they had grown up in, in the washington, dc, brownstone their parents left them, alma painting in the kitchen. maurice became the steward of alma's archive and estate.

and alma thomas was also always a big sister to fannie, the free one, who died of diphtheria before the family migrated from rose hill, georgia, to washington, dc. alma's first preserved work of art is a ceramic bust she made of her sister fannie, the little girl named after grandma in the big bow, the little girl who didn't live long enough to finish elementary school.

is it true that to be a sister to someone who died is like being a sister to someone who was never born? do you have to stretch the canvas. open your arms. extend your reach. become a sister to everyone? generations of shaw junior high students, for example. if you can't see her, who she would have been at this age and this age and this age, do you have to transform what vision means and does, see the unseeable and teach the world to see it too?

this is how i read alma thomas's abstract expressionism. her large-scale paintings. her nurseries and season shifts. her interplanetary view. and i will repeat the seemingly small fact of fannie's death, and alma's decision to represent her in ceramic, and dream next to that representation every night. i will repeat it like alma thomas repeated her brushstrokes, the same color as long as it takes to get across. nothing is small once it reveals a pattern. the potential to change everything. the boldness to reach.

this is what alma thomas is teaching me about method. sister is a form of communication across everything. an audacity.

i have to ignite the surface. expect a full and brazen sky.

# a ceremony for thicker skin

(granddaughter poems)

and then she touched the bloodline with her hands. as red as womb but bigger, flatter. she found the spine of generations and let herself be pulled. until she swam red coral tide, until she breathed acrylic depth. until she couldn't feel the limits of her skin anymore, just what skin held. spilled. offered.

UVA-luminescence image of *Orion*, 1973, which reveals the artist's handprint. National Museum of Women in the Arts, Washington, DC.

# what alma remembers from the dream where her grandparents entertained her at home

in the dream i swirled the land away
like so much paint off my brush in a jar
in the whirlpool of my imagination
the screams reversed
became a song
the song remembered
to be a path
like so much water in the bath
like so much pressure from the sky
i robbed the trees of their gravity
so they could fly
like so many small green birds
with ruby beaks

*Untitled* (*Wooded Landscape*), c. 1952. Oil on canvas, 23 ½ × 22 ½ in. David C. Driskell Center at the University of Maryland, College Park.

# a ceremony for thicker skin

first the red dirt
they let me breathe it
the basins the rags
boiled and scrubbed saturday nights

then the gauntlet of weekday georgia
forcefield training
a repeated decision
to escape the hanging tree
you must grow bark and never bite the hand

the land with all its mineral advice
would line our pores with memories and salt
the lubricated dinners lined us too
warm from the inside

the thin petaled flowers
they planted in a circle
but not before they let me touch
the roots

Reverse of *Antares* (detail revealing canvas and seeping ground), 1972; reverse of *The Eclipse* (detail revealing canvas and seeping ground), 1970. Both Smithsonian American Art Museum, Washington, DC. In Sydney Nikolaus, Gwen Manthey, Melissa Ho, and Amber Kerr, "Composing Color: The Materials and Techniques of Alma Woodsey Thomas," in *Alma W. Thomas: Everything Is Beautiful,* ed. Seth Feman and Jonathan Frederick Walz (Yale University Press, 2021), 98, figs. 6, 7.

# what grandma said

press your back into the tree and listen
when the tree becomes a chair
keep on

who would support your weight
must know
why you haven't yet drowned
in that front yard pool of sunlight
why you haven't yet stopped
  since these trees be galleries of death
why you haven't yet stopped believing

in breath.

*Grandfather's House,* 1952. Oil on canvas, 16 × 20 in. Columbus Museum, GA, Gift of Miss John Maurice Thomas.

# what grandpa said

this is what happened to my blood
it faded and faded until it was everywhere
it spread until it became sky, snow, canvas itself

this is what happened to my blackness
it became the strongest green
i loved it so it grew us our whole world

*Red Tree in High Winter,* 1968. Acrylic and graphite on canvas, 24 × 34 ¼ in. Colby College Museum of Art, Waterville, ME.

behind the platelets, ocean. shadow. behind the shadow, camera. hands. behind the hands, a wandering mind. behind the hands, a bloodfull salted mind.

beneath the clay, water table. life. beneath the life, thirst. memory. beneath the memory, grandpa's yard. circles. beyond the circle, bloodthirsty white people. between the bricks. the flowers push. the petals wake you, don't they.

*Mars Dust,* 1972. Acrylic on canvas, 69 ¼ × 57 ⅛ in. Whitney Museum of American Art, New York.

# field

When Richard Powell, one of the most influential theorists of visual art in the Black diaspora, was a wide-eyed MFA student, or in his sardonic self-description decades later "a young clear-eyed critic striving for objectivity," he wrote a review of Alma Thomas's 1975 exhibition at Howard University.[6] His celebration of Alma Thomas's color paintings may also have been an early critique of other approaches to visual art. Powell the student, knowingly reviewing the work of the first graduate of the very department where he studied, knows that objectivity is impossible for himself or for any of us. He praises Thomas for her choice to "forgo the unreal objectiveness of details and detached photographic realism and dive into what we see and feel."[7] But he also notes that she moves away from what he calls the "mundanity" of impressionism.[8] Instead she "cornrows and parboils it," she "aerates the ground as only a native Georgian can and places growing colors in it the way one plants vegetables and fruit in a backyard."[9] The young Powell prefigures the way that Kellie Jones contextualizes Alma Thomas's experimentalism years later: "Alma Thomas saw herself surrounded by creativity from an early age, from her mother's use of color as an expert seamstress to her extended family's planting and working of southern soil."[10] For both critics, Thomas's roots in and continued connection to the very tangible arts of clothing and feeding people do not contradict but enable the experimental approach that Jones will call "Afro-Futuristic."[11]

When Powell describes Alma Thomas's color fields as "cornrows" he brings to mind two linked references at once: fields of one of the North American continent's most abundant plants, and a beloved and infamous African diasporic hairstyle. Never merely descriptive, Powell's choice of words is also referential. In the first sense cornrows, like other agricultural fields in the United States, share a colonized kinship with the African laborers forced to toil under captivity to generate the vast fields of monocultural crops that continue to define U.S. food systems. In the second sense, cornrows, a time-intensive hairstyle of close braids and patterned open scalp, have been criminalized and forbidden under racist labor codes post-emancipation. But in his positive review, which asserts that there is liberation available to a viewer who chooses to engage Thomas's paintings, he uplifts the brightness and nourishment in her "parboiled" but never overcooked images. Powell does not mean for the reference to cornrows to offer a mere lament for labor. We sense a reclamation in Thomas's paintings and Powell's love for them. Or let me forgo the pretense of objectivity. *I* feel a claim. *I* feel loved. Do you?

Cornrows constitute living archives of sisters and sisterliness. That archive includes my hands in my sister's hair unbraiding it at the end of the summer, my own patience sitting between the legs of my sisterfriend Kara as she parts and flat-twists my hair before our college graduation. The cornrows gracing the heads of people around the world at this moment are mostly the artwork of a diasporic cohort of feminine workers who either offer their craft to people with whom they are in intimate sisterly proximity or with clients to whom they offer their services. Sometimes the line between sister/friend/stylist blurs. Sometimes in the shops staffed by African women and patronized by African American and Afro-Caribbean people in cities in the United States a strained and severed sisterhood across diasporic difference reveals or rejects a longing for tenderness among the tender-headed, tenderhearted, and tense. I would suggest that all of these braiders are modeling the work of sistering, the generative challenge of the closest simultaneous interfaces of similarity and difference.

John Maurice Thomas, Alma's younger sister, who usually went by "Maurice" and lived in the same Washington, DC, house with Alma their whole adult lives, practiced parting, styling, and threading in her work as an archivist and curator of her older sister's work and legacy. Her institutional choices of where to place certain artifacts, and especially her penciled notes on the backs of pictures and event programs clarifying Alma's presence and achievements, have the tight, gentle touch of a person accountable for preserving an intimate witness, a close deviation from her own life.

Alma Thomas, who lived inside the practice of sistering and lives today as a result of the archival and curatorial care of her younger sister, becomes related to and different from generations of braiders. Her bright brushstrokes and the spaces between them, Powell suggests with his cornrow reference, do not only beckon our minds, they open up our crowns.

When I first heard Malcolm Peacock's voice, he was running. His words punctuated by the need for breath, ragged and reaching like the closest view of the spaces between Alma Thomas's applications of color. In his recorded reflections while running, the reach for breath shapes the insights Peacock shares about life, love, racism, intimacy, and Hortense Spillers, among other topics. We feel the breath that disrupts and enables each articulation at the same moment. When I actually talked to Malcolm on the phone, their voice was steadier. They were sitting still and explaining how these days they were walking from Brooklyn to Harlem every day, past Teachers College, where Alma Thomas studied, up to the Studio Museum's transitional studio space, where they were applying their mother's living room cornrow technique to the task of braiding together a redwood tree. Malcolm texted me a photograph of their studio floor covered with packets of hair extensions and noted that their marathon braiding sessions kept them up in Harlem in vigil with countless African hair-braiding establishments finishing one or two last clients late into the night.[12]

As far as I know, Alma Thomas doesn't have a painting of corn in particular or of the redwoods where Malcolm Peacock once ran a last-minute marathon while fearing for his Black life. But her paintings do evoke corn in their patterned multiplicity. We could think of her color paintings both as fields of corn in rows, and as each ear of corn, kernel after indented kernel, holding close and sweet. The heirloom Cherokee corn I help grow and harvest at Tierra Negra Farm near my home in Durham, North Carolina, does what Alma does. It places different colors in tight kerneled relationship to each other across a field of possibility. When we shuck the corn we are surprised by each ear because no pattern is the same. This one has purple blue magenta maroon kernels alternating. This one has all purple and one white. Most of them look like an autumn rainbow, but never the same rainbow twice. The cornrows of an Alma Thomas painting both look like the infinitely diverse ears of native corn and hold the ethic of the Indigenous context of corn that is, again, sisterhood. Just as Alma Thomas's paintings exceed the monotony of agribusiness conformity in their movement and flow, corn on this continent is meant to exist in mounds as part of the three sisters Indigenous planting system. As Potawatomi scientist and poet Robin Wall Kimmerer describes it, corn is the oldest sister, sprouting up first out of the ground, followed by the second sister, the beans that climb the cornstalks encircling her. Then the sprawl of squash leaves and flowers sitting on the ground at their feet skirts them both, filling in almost all of the available space between mound after mound of earth, each about a square foot wide.[13] Alma Thomas reveals herself as kin again not only through her grandmother Fannie Simmons, a South Carolinian woman of African, Indigenous, and European heritage, but also in practice, offering mark after mark in the tradition of the Indigenous farmers who create not merely furrowed linear rows of earth but constellations of mounds so the three dimensions of the intertwined plants can fill the space, feed the people, nourish the land, open the earth to the lessons of rain.

During a conversation I did not directly witness, my old friend Ashon Crawley, who makes paintings that are the remnants of his embodied sound work in the tradition of Black Pentecostal breathing, told my new friend, the world-building critical writer Sofia Samatar, that his paintings, records of what happens on the floor while he moves in the sound and spirit of transforming a homophobic tradition into a vessel of queer possibility, were not landscape paintings. And in the sense of the colonial optic of landscape painting as a form of domination and ownership over living space, of course they are not. But Sofia offered a corrective that Ashon included in one of the letters in his book *The Lonely Letters* about what landscape might be. And I think Sofia might know, since she writes books with maps in the beginning so we can find ourselves inside the worlds she has created and populated with her own reflective imagination. Sofia said Ashon's paintings are landscapes in the sense that they invite the maroon questions, *Can I shelter there? Can I get in there? Can I stay there for a while?*

Sofia calls this "landscape from the inside" because it is about inhabiting a space.[14] I would add that it is a vulnerable form of inhabitation; there is need and precarity there. Ashon explains that in his painting practice he is trying to get back into, to shelter within, the sound of the Black church, his community of aesthetic origin, a homophobic community that excluded him even while he, as a prolific church organist, was providing the context, the sound of that community's being. *Can I shelter there? Can I stay?*

Was Alma Thomas a maroon? She was not housing insecure. She lived her adult life in a house her parents purchased that she and her sister inherited together. She was gainfully employed, an active and respected member of her church and community. If we think of Alma Thomas as a maroon, we have to imagine her marooned in time. What if the "achievement" of being first is simply the consistent pattern of arriving where no one expects you? Of enacting things no one has found a use or a name for until you insist? What if Alma Thomas, marveled at in the *New York Times,* the *New Yorker,* and the *Washington Evening Star* as an old new young artist after retiring from teaching, was marooned in age? Alma's painting teacher says that in her arthritic last days she would cry out, "Oh if I only had a body!" When she went to the hospital to what would be her deathbed, she brought her paints with her.[15] What if Alma Thomas was marooned in space too? Committed to uplifting her Washington, DC, community while longing for a Georgia she returned to most frequently in paintings? Marooned in the early dream of a world where her students could live with dignity? A world safe enough for her sister Fannie to have had the equal medical access that would have allowed her to live through childhood into adulthood? What if Alma Thomas's paintings are imagined landscapes where the movement of the air and the movement of time create a maroonage, a free place, where linear time loops back? Where a girl from the horse and buggy age can travel to the moon and Mars without leaving what and whom she loves behind? What if the vulnerable question of shelter is a question about whether she can access her dead baby sister's heaven? Can that space hold her? Does it still hold their relationship?

Can I get in there? It could be a question about seeking to reach a sound, a feeling, a possible world beyond our undoing. Can I shelter there? It could be a question about what will hold, what will hold me. Can I stay? At least for a while? It could be a longing across impermanence. It could be my question each time I am faced with the full and open world of Thomas's paintings. Can I get to the world that her work implies? Can it hold me? And what does that work have to say about the world I see when I reach, when I'm vulnerable, when I close my eyes and remember there is a landscape inside?

Thomas's works, often inspired by her own garden and the gardens of others, or fields and seasons and the emergence of flowers and the changing of leaves and images of outer space, are all spatial and temporal. They are about time and space, but they do not fix a given space in time. They offer repetition and difference. They offer proximity and contrast. They offer the phenomena she witnesses, the freedom of presence. They cultivate possibility. They create a possible encounter between Alma Thomas and a viewer, this viewer, any viewer, between an image Alma Thomas blinked inside and a future in which dead Alma Thomas is a presence. They create a possible encounter between a living Alma Thomas and her sister Fannie who was already pure spirit and also therefore between modes of encounter. What is at stake in my encounter with this work?

Consider Rick Powell's description of Alma Thomas's 1968 painting *Orange Glow* during his series of Mellon Lectures at the National Gallery in Thomas's hometown of Washington, DC. It's so beautiful, it's like a spell. He names the "harmonious optics" of the primary, secondary, and tertiary color choices and then remarks on points where they "bust loose."[16] He riffs on the "radiant and vibrant connotations" of the title *Orange Glow* and how orange, a minority color in the painting, modifies the prioritized glow of Thomas's intuitively placed colors, suggesting that the orange colors in the painting also "transform everything in their orbit."[17] He keeps going to the cosmic, understanding that the glow referenced in the title and enacted in the painting, "not unlike sunlight, envelops nature and civilization and covered Thomas's gritty inner-city neighborhood with brilliance and optimism."[18] He branches out to her other paintings of flowers and nurseries, her documentation of "planet earth's chromatic responses to seasonal and atmospheric cycles."[19]

He quotes the Black British Guyanese artist Frank Bowling on color as line and applies Bowling's observation that incorporating line between the colors introduces clashes "wherever the colors meet in a confused passion."[20] As a Caribbean immigrant to the United Kingdom, Bowling knows of what he speaks. Powell continues emphasizing again the "abstract cornrows and plait-like gestures,"[21] the "light and energy generating ideal," the passion, the confusion that happens when I see you in a different light.[22]

I don't think that I will ever describe Alma Thomas's paintings better than Rick Powell already has. Not even a 1975 student Rick Powell.

Certainly not a Mellon Distinguished Lecturer Rick Powell. Thankfully, I'm not trying to.

Alma Thomas and the artists I have named here (Powell included!) are all in the midst of transforming a deadly encounter, the genocidal colonial encounter, the earth-killing monocultural agricultural domination, the reproduction of property through landscape painting, the reification of art as property through art criticism. I think Powell's approach here and elsewhere points us in this liberatory direction. My encounter with Alma Thomas's work wants to do this too. But my mode is different.

Instead of describing the work and then describing it better, or more pointedly, instead of demonstrating mastery or conferring mastery upon the artist, I have to risk freedom. I have to confront sameness and difference. I have to confront what I mean when what I want to be the same is different and what I wish were different reproduces itself and stays the same. I have to be transformed by how I see myself and lose myself in you. I have to risk another form of knowing. I have to refuse to master. Goldenrod. Aster. I have to refuse to daughter. Dirt. Water. Rain barrel cistern. I have to become related alongside you. Woven with you. Unraveling too. I have to sister.

If I were to attempt to describe Alma Thomas's 1973 painting *Jonquils* in the mode of art critical inquiry, I would try to find words for that exact yellow. Is it goldenrod or should I not use another flower to describe a flower? Is it a gold yellow, a light yellow, a light-infused yellow? And then I would seek to tell you how the strokes of yellow meet, crash into each other, crowd each other, embrace each other in some places, overlap and darken each other in other places. And they could look like scattered grains of corn from some angles. But to me these brushstrokes mostly look like living beings moved by wind. And in the end, I am too awestruck by how she has infused the inert with movement again to say anything else, except maybe death, where is thy victory? Segregation, proffer your concession call? And so in the end, I am not at the end. I am moved, beyond my lifetime. I am opened into the sistering relation of crowding or embracing. I should know what you are thinking and I will never understand you. The decoloniality is: that this relation remains a question, not a relation of domination or reproduction but of accompaniment, or betrayal, solidarity, or judgment across something and something else. I wonder about you. I lean back and look again.

What does a sistering relation or the loss of it make possible? I continue in wonder and build a room to ponder the motivation of a genius who has created not only a work of art, but a transformation of what work even is or could be or could become in the face of death. And for whom? The question is *can we stay here?* And the answer is no. And the answer is yes. And this is the poem:

SISTER TECH

i am pounding out a field of gold
with a horsehair hammer
the interface i use to build
this, our cosmic computer

with a horsehair hammer
and the light of memory
our cosmic computer
creates a circuit between worlds

and the light of memory
and your unforgettable face
and a circuit between worlds
your hand to my hand

and your face behind my eyelids
and all the flowers
are your hands
too soon they freeze and die

and oh the flowers
become my faith
too soon
we pound the earth

break into gold

*Jonquils,* 1973. Acrylic on canvas, 26 × 36 ½ in. Michael Rosenfeld Gallery, New York.

# studies in sistering

# fannie

there are this many pieces of me. smeared blood. sunrise. soil. clay. sand. plaster. there are this many edges of me. bile. lipstick. the innards of fireflies. remnants of dinner. rust at the edge of the porch. there are just so many ways to shade the instances of light that weigh my neck, press down my shoulders, open my eyes too far to see anything but what moths see while they eat their way through. there are this many versions of you falling out of me. wet leaves of leaving. wet face of waking up without you in my hands. there are only so many ways to say i need you. oil. paint. fire. land. i miss you every piece of every day.

*Female Nude Standing,* 1950s. Oil on canvas, 40 ½ × 24 ⅝ in. La Salle University Art Museum, Philadelphia.

# love comes down

love comes down
from the sky
through the sky
as the sky
all spectrum

and refraction

i can catch it
i can catch it

rainbow it back
to you.

Poster for the Franz Bader Gallery exhibition *Alma Thomas: Earth and Space Paintings*, 1970. Photomechanical reproduction. Smithsonian American Art Museum, Washington, DC.

# one day

one day i tried to piece sky together with sky
building a ladder to where you are
and every piece was sharp in my hands
every minute thin but nothing broke
more than it was already broken
and so i gave the break back to the sky
and when you gonna
climb down

tomorrow?

*Untitled*, c. 1963. Painted metal and wire, 74 × 48 × 4 in. Charles Thomas Lewis, promised gift to the Columbus Museum, GA.

# method

this is how i build your heaven
one brick at a time
where a brick is a day
and a day is a brush across

one brick at a time
and the sunrise could mean anything
and a day is a brush across
galaxies

and the sunrise could mean anything
and the ocean waits to catch you
i travel to galaxies
where you still exist

and the ocean waits to catch you
in my eyes
you still exist
in my hands

in my eyes
where a brick is a day
build your heaven
with both hands

*Apollo 12 "Splash Down,"* 1970. Acrylic and graphite on canvas, 50 ¼ × 50 ¼ in. Tang Teaching Museum and Art Gallery, Saratoga Springs, NY.

# study in sistering

this is how light works
your face my face
lean back into the triangle of sun
and reach don't look away

your face my face
our tilted heads one smile
reach don't look away
how much i love you

our tilted heads one smile
framed by the green that knows
how much i love you
a million leaves

framed by the green that knows
i am never leaving
a million leaves
a million stays

i am never leaving
lean back into the triangle of sun
a million stitches fill the day
that's how light works

*Alma and Sister Maurice,* 1922/23. Photograph. Caption by John Maurice Thomas: "Alma and Sister Maurice. The costume made and designed by my Mother. Picture made in the back yard of our home in DC." Collection of the Columbus Museum, GA.

# reason

i will be your elephant. face paint. bruise,
i will be your most vulnerable memory.
i will be your grass stain. picked scab. move.
teaching you what won't
ever wash away.

i will be your cotton candy. cheap prize. blush.
i will be your best day at the fair.
i will be your purple tongue, falling ladder. crooked earth.

your reason to stay.

Side-by-side details of *Autumn Drama,* 1969, under infrared and normal light showing revised color annotations. In Seth Feman and Jonathan Frederick Walz, eds., *Alma W. Thomas: Everything Is Beautiful* (Yale University Press, 2021), 97.

# on color

if eventually. we all fade to bone. we all become fossil. impossible clay.
then let's ask today what color. what broken fading color. what tragically
    temporary color shall we be.
if at last. we all fall through earth. we all reverse birth. all fold back in.
then where shall i put my red yellow blues. my ridiculous shoes. my
    purse made for nothing.
because yes. we will all fade to blessed. unknown. unguessed. like the
    taste of this dress.

Brochure for the Whitney Museum of American Art exhibition *Alma W. Thomas,* 1972. Alma Thomas Papers, Columbus Museum, GA.

# the burnt regreening

black love

*in the middle?*
*coral singing my name*
*pangea outside your window*

*in my dream*
*you are never an oil spill*
*in my dream*
*you are never a blight*

*at the edges?*
*the clouds of a ghost building*
*hello ancestral smog*

*in my eyes*
*you are wilder than a billionaire*
*in my heart*
*much more familiar than a frog*

*so if black*
*is the burnt regreening*
*or if black*
*is the people well*
*or if coal*
*is the place for keeping*
*the mineral swell*

*i wish you breath*
*i wish you home*
*i wish you flight*
*i wish you bell*

*Transcendental,* 1963/65. Watercolor on paper, 22 × 28 in. Charles Thomas Lewis Collection.

In *Art on My Mind,* bell hooks generates a Black feminist art theoretical practice out of her critiques of what she views as the misreadings, underratings, and decontextualizations of works and practices of Black visual artists that are important to her. The work and life of Alma Thomas are important to me. And in the face of an art critical tradition that I will mostly not rehearse here, which has named the abstract expressionist turn in the work of Alma Thomas as a turn to the apolitical, I dress myself in the lamentation that bell hooks offered in response to the early reception of the work of her friend the artist Alison Saar: "She did not contemplate the reality that no critical framework existed to theoretically validate and illuminate the significance of this shift, its political subversiveness."[23] I need a framework not only cognizant of the context of Thomas's world and the interpretive context that overdetermines Black expression, but also a mode that honors the criticality of a range of practices.

When Jonathan P. Binstock describes Alma Thomas as an "apolitically intentioned" artist in his essay "Apolitical Art in a Political World: Alma Thomas in the Late 1960s and Early 1970s," he is offering a definition of the political that is too narrow for the work that I do here, or indeed for my very existence.[24] I need bell hooks, who insists that the very practice of Black artists making space not only for their own visions, but also for the practices of freedom they may find in the very creation of art, has major political stakes and is itself a critical intervention. As she explains, "Studying the history of painting by African-Americans, one sees that abstract expressionism influenced the development of many artists precisely because *it was a critical intervention,* an expansion of a closed turf. It was a site of possibility."[25]

Faith Ringgold, a Black woman artist whom critics acknowledge as unquestionably political due to her work as an activist disrupting racist institutions, and her use of text and direct engagement with stereotypes to provide freedom narratives, seems to dismiss Thomas's whole generation of Black artists for describing their art in universalist terms. In her essay "The 1960s: Is There a Black Art?" she contrasts her own unapologetically Black approach to what she describes as "half-stepping" by an earlier generation of artists:

> Art for them was an abstraction, a fragment of an idea that nobody could understand, much less condemn. However, I had called

my art "Super Realism" because I wanted my audience to make a personal connection with its image and the message. The older artists were cautious—"half-stepping" as they used to say in the sixties—trying to get by in the art world and not drawing attention to their blackness. "Art is art. Quality is the important thing. It doesn't matter what color you are" was their message. They knew there was little or no support for artists in the black community—so what could be gained by alienating friends and contacts in the white art world?[26]

Ringgold describes this type of claim to universality as a pragmatic move by artists who knew the limitations of a racist art world. And Thomas did insist on the quality of her own art in race-transcendent terms: "Creative art is for all time and is therefore independent of time," she insisted in the same interview where Mahal asked her about inhumanity. "It is of all ages, of every land, and if by this we mean that the creative spirit in man which produces a picture or a statue is common to the whole civilized world, independent of age, race and nationality, the statement may stand."[27]

In her essay "To the Max: Energy and Experimentation," Kellie Jones describes Thomas as having an "Afro-Futuristic" approach because of her interest in space travel in her later paintings and the way "she imagined seeing her visions of earthbound flora from 'way up there on the moon' or 'planes that are airborne' as well, even before having flown commercially, which signaled her progressive, forward-looking vision or Afro-Futuristic thinking."[28] Maybe Thomas's universalism is not the colonial universalism of a Western gaze, but rather a Black woman's revolutionary act of filling the universe with her freedom.

There is no true binary between Ringgold and Thomas. Ringgold ultimately does not actually discard the generation of Black artists who came before her, or any generation of Black artists past or future. In fact, later in the same memoir where she notes the "half-stepping" of the abstract artists of Thomas's generation, Ringgold reveals that Alma Thomas was one of the artists whose work she was sure to bring to students when she began to teach the history of Black art in her early job at Wagner College on Staten Island.[29] Ringgold, like Thomas, taught for decades in the public school system and centered Black children for much of her artistic production. Sometimes I see Alma Thomas in Faith

Ringgold's children's books. In Ringgold's book *Dinner at Aunt Connie's House,* we follow a young girl who looks at portraits of Black women historical figures on the wall of her aunt's home. Behind the portraits are moving lines of rainbow colors. Would they appear in an Alma Thomas mode if we zoomed in? In her classic *Tar Beach,* Ringgold's character Cassie Lightfoot flies above the earth seeking to rectify the injustice of racism on behalf of her family. How similar is her view of earth to Alma Thomas's sky blur?

A view of an earth alive. In motion. Reclaimed.

Not everyone would view Alma Thomas's approach as pragmatic. And she did alienate some people, according to her friend the brilliant Black printmaker Lou Stovall: "There was a lot of, 'Who does Alma think she is, and what does she think she's doing?' Here is this little lady and she is painting on the edge, and people would think, 'How can she paint on the edge if she's already outside?'"[30] And Thomas herself told her former professor Jacob Kainen that she worried when she thought her work was too "user friendly" in a racist market.[31] I would not describe Thomas's relationship to abstraction as cautious. I would also not describe her claim to universalism as cautious. I would put it alongside the way bell hooks describes "the days when I thought of art only as the expressive activity of a soul struggling to self-actualize. Art has no race or gender. Art, and most especially painting, was for me a realm where every imposed boundary could be transgressed. It was the free world of color where all was possible."[32]

Alma Thomas's work transgressed imposed boundaries and insisted on a context where all things were possible. Her description of "the creative spirit" as something that is common in all people across time prefigures June Jordan's concept in her essay "The Creative Spirit," which proclaims, "I believe that the creative spirit is nothing less than love made manifest."[33] Jordan goes on to explain that this creative spirit exists most certainly across age and should inform our ethic of intergenerational engagement; but she also wants us to know that the creative spirit is shared within all life, most notably for Jordan, and seemingly for Thomas, in the blooming flowers.

In the circle of the poplars, in sight of the spiral flower beds, bleeding out of the red clay of Rose Hill, Georgia, Alma Thomas experienced a robust intergenerational educational community as a young girl. Her mother the seamstress, her aunts the teachers, the brilliant friends, scholars, and artists, many of them Tuskegee graduates, all gathered in Alma's grandparents' living room and read and discussed textbooks on literature and empire, Europe and Rome. A Howard grad came and taught painting lessons on velvet canvases. Alma remembers that a white professor even came in from Atlanta at least once a month, and this is in addition to the activities of the organizations her parents belonged to—her father was a Mason, her mother was of the Order of the Eastern Star. What Thomas later called "cultural clubs" dreamed and debated beauty and consequence while outside racial terror spat and started whenever Black folks did anything too beautiful or too consequential.[34]

And yet here goes Alma. Creating with consequence through to her last breath. Devoting herself to impact generations of Black children surviving segregation. Standing on the kitchen chair, tying brushes to herself despite her arthritis, determined to create works that were energetic and unforgettable. Could that ever be apolitical? The Black feminist poet Ntozake Shange describes a childhood similar to Thomas's generations later. She notes that she grew up in a segregated Black community in St. Louis with creative parents, a father who painted, a mother who hosted Black artists, musicians, writers, and thinkers from all over the world in their living room. Her father collected Afro-diasporic drums. Her mother recited Harlem Renaissance poetry. Years later she said of her segregated growing up, "I was raised in absolutely colored neighborhoods . . . so it never occurred to me that we were illegitimate in some way because we were a whole world."[35] It was when Shange was put on a bus as a "gifted" child to integrate a mostly white school that she experienced daily bullying and a complete dissociation from her educational experience. She knew how to access love though: "I surrounded myself in images, abstractions that drew warmth from me or wrapped me in loveliness. . . . Loving someone to me, at one point, meant enveloping them in beauty: smells, visions, textures, me. Later I discovered that one must challenge in loving as in life."[36] Marooned in Texas, where she could not find the art galleries that supported her spirit, Shange decided to write *Ridin' the Moon in Texas: Word Paintings,* a book of ekphrastic poems in conversation with visual artworks, to reground herself in the creative environment of her first home, with a focus on abstract images.

Am I acting on a similar impulse? In the poems that follow, I write about Alma Thomas in a Black feminist first person. This is a transformative first person as theorized by the poet and scholar

Evie Shockley. Shockley, who has also written a phenomenal poem engaging Alma Thomas's *Starry Night and the Astronauts,* describes herself as someone who "writes thinks and creates with her eye on a Black feminist horizon."[37] And so of course she would look towards Alma Thomas's oceanic earth and brightening sky. In her talk "When and Where 'I' Enters," Shockley contextualizes the Black feminist first person in a tradition emphasizing Anna Julia Cooper, whose statement "When and where I enter . . . the whole race enters with me," from her book *A Voice from the South,* is a founding Black feminist reference and the inspiration for the title of historian Paula Giddings's influential work *When and Where I Enter: The Impact of Black Women on Race and Sex in America.* Shockley charts how Cooper, Giddings, Gwendolyn Brooks, Patricia J. Williams, Harryette Mullen, and even Alexis Pauline Gumbs use the personal pronoun in ways that problematize the assumption of direct representationality or universal individualism in the use of "I."[38] Instead there is a geometry of distance, perspective, and movement that offers a transformative critical relation. In her poem "alma's arkestral vision (or farther out)," Shockley practices play with pronouns, never using "I" but finding the "we" in "u" and "you" and "us." Shockley's multi-movement poem moves with Thomas, putting her painting in conversation with the work of Sun Ra's Arkestra, a move that feels resonant with Thomas, who listened to a wide range of music while she painted. I cannot describe Shockley's poem even close to as beautifully as she poems it, because the poem itself is visual art. For example, the first movement of the poem uses the word "you" like a brushstroke, repeating it and shaping it until it becomes a large "we" on the page. In the ninth and last movement, Shockley describes the perspective of the one who sees. Maybe Alma Thomas, maybe Fannie, maybe God.

> she sees us
> each streak of color[39]

And then the poet paints again, shaping the repeating word "we" into a large letter "u," which serves as the shared first letter for the first and last words in the phrase "unique in the universe." Or because of the way it lines up, you could read it "wenique in the weniverse." Again, Alma Thomas inspires a transformed relationship to the universe we find in relation.

The first person of this next set of poems, imagined artist statements, does not have to represent. First of all, Alma Thomas does not have anything to prove. I live in a time where Black feminist thinkers like Kellie Jones and Evie Shockley are thinking about and writing with Alma Thomas's body of work. And I do not have to represent Alma Thomas. The first person of these poems could be Thomas or a larger or smaller or living or dead or dispersed or unifying creator. I am engaging Alma Thomas's works and artifacts in a world of Black aliveness, like the world Kevin Quashie creates for Black poetry and essays in his study of the same name. Not a world of universalism but a universe where black is a free relation, free to express and revise and wonder. Quashie says, "If I could, I would have called this book 'Aliveness.' If I could, I would have dropped the qualifier; I could speak of us—of any one of black us—as being of aliveness and it would be discursively self-evident. . . . If I could, this book would not need to exist."[40] Quashie's beautiful study of, not merely coincidentally, many of my own favorite writers models a reading practice that operates "as if" the white gaze and our traumatic experience of it were not reproducing blackness as abjection all around us. As if Thomas's childhood living room, Ntozake Shange's childhood living room, June Jordan's living room, my own living room were the whole world. They are not. And the living rooms of many people who own works by Alma Thomas are not sanctuaries for actual Black aliveness. But that aliveness does exist in the space of the paintings and the poems and the practice of prioritizing an idea of beauty that is free of imposed boundaries. It does exist in the legacy of the woman who founded a "beauty club" sponsored by her church to teach the children of her neighborhood to see beauty in themselves and their community during her time "off" from teaching art. This is the freedom that Quashie insists on when he says, "We are not the idea of us, not even the idea that we hold of us. We are us, multiple and varied, becoming. The heterogeneity of us. Blackness in a black world is everything, which means it gets to be freed from being any one thing. We are ordinary beauty, black people, and beauty must be allowed to do its beautiful work."[41]

# artist statements

sometimes the chalk lines come back. dotted on mother's fabric. gliding across my chalkboard. shaped like someone on this bitter asphalt earth. writing in stardust. an erasable almost breathable white across color. in my dreams i find my way across the red sea in powdered sand like chalk dust. in my daydreams i don't talk. i paint.

*Untitled* (*Music Series*) (detail showing white paint retouching), 1978. Smithsonian American Art Museum, Washington, DC.

# ready

in my dream i became paint
blended ready
applied to the task
only slightly bleeding into

only slightly bleeding into
the student next to me
blended ready
our mixedrace blackness

our race people black list
of talents and skills
students together
imperative

imperative
collection
of talents and skills
to survive this world we made

to survive this world we made
for free
collected
in bondage

in bondage
applied to the task
of freedom
in the dream

i was blood sweat and tears

*Art School,* Howard University Yearbook ("The Bison"), 1923.

# circular frame

from here i can see you
round as wanting
scope of my open mouth
from here i can hold you

round as wanting
old as air
from here i can hold you
and breathe

old as air
inherit blink
and breathe
and understand

inherit blink
and capture light
and understand
my place

and capture light
in your face
and spin out of
my place

in your face
my scope my open mouth
spin out
from here

Pete Copeland, *American Art Goes to Africa*, 1973. Black-and-white photograph. George Washington University, Special Collections Research Center, Corcoran Gallery of Art and Corcoran College of Art and Design, Washington, DC. Alma Thomas took a trip to Tanzania from September 8 to October 15, 1972. Adolphus Ealey, director of the Barnett-Aden Collection, is showing Thomas and Adele Rogers, the wife of the secretary of state, the selection of Black art in the U.S. Embassy. In Seth Feman and Jonathan Frederick Walz, eds., *Alma W. Thomas: Everything Is Beautiful* (Yale University Press, 2021), 178.

# study

i give you now
the regions of my heart
quadrant of sky
corner of red
epoch of sun
returning shade
the way light falls
on my open chest
is study

the book in my hand
the dip of my blouse
the blood of my skirt
my face turning gold
what i drop
where i lean
what i hold
study that

infinity of skin
enclosure of hair
unfinished hands
red everywhere red
there's your evidence.

*Study of a Young Woman,* c. 1955. Oil on fiberboard, 35 ¾ × 27 ¾ in. Robert L. Johnson from the Barnett-Aden Collection, Washington, DC.

# bright

i made myself from misrecognition
stacked your traditions on their heads
i lift a cloud of false predictions
with this miraculous neck

stacking renditions
i head toward perdition
this neck a miracle
this tongue a song

i lose my head
in the brilliant instead
sweet as sunday
brushes strong

brush the blue
out the heavens
save it save it
bright as god

Ida Jervis, *Alma Thomas at Home,* 1968. Gelatin silver print. Alma Thomas Papers, c. 1894–2001, Of Alma Thomas, 1950s–60s, box 5, folder 36, Archives of American Art, Smithsonian Institution, Washington, DC.

Unknown photographer, *Portrait of Alma Thomas,* undated. Gelatin silver print. Columbus Museum, GA, Gift of Miss John Maurice Thomas in memory of her parents, John H. and Amelia W. Cantey Thomas.

# memo

there are bursts of light
where the wall doesn't touch
the ceiling

there are corners
and ways you will not
see

there are images
of the broken floor
the falling sky

you will only know
if i frame them
prop them up

there are truths

they will only find you
if you stand back

and watch me work

Edward Peterson, Installation view of *Alma Thomas: Recent Paintings 1975–1976*, 1976, at Martha Jackson West. Martha Jackson Gallery Archives, University at Buffalo Art Galleries, State University of New York at Buffalo.

# joy: assignment for the beauty club before graduation

all the flower petals in the world
gather them up
release them
whisper
your secret
to each and every one

all the fallen leaves that ever fell
gather them
crunch them in your hands
tell them what you know
about love in wintertime

every tube of lipstick
every trace of blood
juice-stained t-shirt
discarded jelly packet
flattened bug

whatever you find
give it what you learned
from me

*Falling Leaves, Love Wind Orchestra,* 1977. Acrylic on canvas, 21 ½ × 27 ½ in. Private collection.

# birthday blues

what else blooms
out my hands for you
what else stains
the day
how else love
gonna get to you
what
other
way

Cover of a birthday card, early 1960s. Watercolor on paper, 7 × 5 in. (closed). Columbus Museum, GA, Gift of Miss John Maurice Thomas in memory of her parents, John H. and Amelia W. Cantey Thomas.

# instructions

if i should ever sleep
surround me in my own stain
evidence of the salt i had to share
the oil i let my smallest joints release
then cover me in acrylic
the birds will never know
i don't have wings
wrap me in my vapors
the bluest cloth
my mother ever touched
it's not too much
to dip me in an ocean
round enough to cradle
gasping songs
rock me in a wood frame
splintered in my own stain
if i ever ever fall
asleep

Roland Freeman, *Alma Thomas's Bedroom*, 1973. Digital scan of a color transparency. Collection of Roland Freeman.

# short bio

from the crowded blues
out walked my joy
up rose my joy
so bright you can't miss it
so big you can have some too

*Untitled* (*Double Sided, Side 1*), 1960s. Watercolor on paper, 14 × 16 ½ in. Columbus Museum, GA, Gift of Miss John Maurice Thomas in memory of her parents, John H. and Amelia W. Cantey Thomas.

# free all necks

# free all necks

## *1: Fabric*

At the end of her life Alma Thomas insisted: "People always want to cite me for my color paintings, but I would much rather be remembered for having laid a foundation for children's lives."[42]

In 1935, at the age of forty-three, during a summer off from teaching art at Shaw Junior High School in segregated Washington, DC, she took an intensive course with Tony Sarg, often called the "father of American puppetry," in New York City.[43] The class entailed "one hundred hours of instruction in every phase of the Marionette Theatre."[44] A year before, in her master's thesis for her degree in arts education from Columbia University's Teachers College, Alma had argued that the creation of a marionette theater could bring together multiple educational subjects for her students.[45] It could also offer a beautiful way to bring her earlier work, as a costume designer for the Howard Players (the drama troupe at her beloved alma mater), into her creative educational practice.

The students, Alma reasoned, would learn history while researching the characters, learn design and color theory while creating the costumes, learn shop while building and lighting the stage, learn writing while crafting the dialogue, learn drama while acting out the plays, and learn civic responsibility while reaching out to the community to attend their shows. And what did they learn while creating small people from fabric and stuffing, stringing them up from a wooden platform they had built? They learned how to animate life on their own terms.

They say that by the time Alma Thomas retired from teaching at Shaw Junior High School in 1960, at least half of DC's Black community had been her students. There is a power in being first. An even greater power in lasting. What does it mean that in the land of political puppets, a woman born in Georgia at the high-water mark of U.S. mob lynchings taught her students to saw the wood, connect the strings, bring joy and laughter to their families and communities by giving life to hanging dolls year after year?

Could I learn that?

*2: Wood*

Rose Hill, Georgia. 1891. Every breath a prayer. Amelia Thomas was shaking. Would that she could be as rooted as a poplar, but she had to be ready to run. Big with her first child, she prayed that the men with dogs and ropes would pass by, disperse, give up, go away. Eventually, the Georgia trees received her anxious prayers, breathed in her carbon dioxide pleas, and used them to whisper their own wonderings. What tree would the mob choose next? Which of their limbs would be desecrated by the cruel white supremacist enforcement of "man's inhumanity to man"?[46]

Amelia survived that night in Rose Hill. But when she gave her soul to light, birthed Alma, her first child, and sang to soothe her brown baby's dreams, she noticed that her daughter was born hard of hearing. Her fear, Amelia believed, transmitted through amniotic fluid, had blocked her baby's listening ears. Even before she was born, Alma had heard too much.

Alma Thomas left Georgia with her family as a child because there were no high schools that would admit a colored girl. And since her Mama Amelia already knew the sound of the Atlanta race riots, which broke out on Alma's fifteenth birthday, she said *no more* to white men once again roaming with dogs and weapons, seeking whatever lost parts of their souls they had bartered to whiteness. "Take off your shoes and shake all that Georgia sand out of them and don't look back," she told her daughters when they got to Washington, DC.[47]

But Alma did look back.

The trees were still beckoning. And the land held more than memories of segregation and racial terror; it also held the short life of Alma's younger sister Fannie, who died of diphtheria in the early 1900s at ten years old. Fannie was the subject of Alma's first sculpture, which she kept in her room, next to her bed, for the rest of her days. Maybe that's why Alma never stopped painting those flowerbeds of Rose Hill, those elder poplar trees.

*3: Paint*

We know that Alma Thomas's commitment to her students' education—a level of education that Fannie didn't live to participate in—was profound. She not only taught them during the week; she also organized after-school and Saturday trips to museums and a "beauty club," based on the philosophy that they would need to learn to see beauty in their own community, in themselves. Therefore, I think Alma Thomas thought about the necks of her students as she taught them to hold their heads up higher. I believe that as she taught them to stuff and stitch marionettes together, she hoped that they would learn what they were made of and what they could create. This is the woman who said, of her largest painting, *Red Azaleas Singing and Dancing to Rock and Roll Music,* "Do you see that painting? Look at it move. That's energy. And I'm the one who put it there. I transform energy with these old limbs of mine."[48]

### *4: Strings*

But what is the relationship between a puppet and a Black child in the early twentieth century, or a puppet and a Black grown woman in the early twenty-first century, for that matter? I kept looking at the materials listed in the caption for an image of a marionette Thomas made: "fabric, wood, paint and strings."[49] What am I made of, I wondered? And so, for the summer of my year of Alma Thomas, the first hour of my day, eventually approximately one hundred hours total, I wrote a series of poems where the title is that caption. I looked at the educational encounters in my own life (broadly speaking, because isn't birth an education? isn't being my father's daughter or my sister's sister an educational experience?) and asked myself a series of questions:

> What is the fabric?
> What is the wood?
> What is the paint?
> What are the strings?

I surrendered to the possibility that I might learn about a variety of subjects if I asked these questions again and again. All summer.

# fabric, wood, paint, and strings (our savior lutheran c. 1992)

pleated tunic
corner computer
marvel mutants
failing names

sharp nails
ready knuckles
oregon trail
tether ball twine

fire
glasses
smarts
the only one

When my family moved to South Florida in 1992, it wasn't to escape racism. In fact, in order to be closer to my mother's family after my parents got divorced, we moved to a town called Plantation. Was this name an accurate marker of what the land had been or a nostalgic predictor of what white people moving to newly developed apartment complexes and subdivisions might have longed for? I still don't know.

If we had stayed in New Jersey, I would have started middle school, but in Broward County I still had one more year of elementary school to go, and so my sister and I both went to Our Savior Lutheran, a small school attached to a church we did not attend, where we had to wear navy-blue tunics and penny loafers. I was the only Black girl in my grade. My sister and I may have been the only Black girls in the whole school. I remember playing four square and tetherball and hanging upside down from the monkey bars in the colorful shorts I learned to conceal under my uniform. I remember that the X-Men were popular, but I don't think my classmates liked them for the reasons I liked them. I thought I must be made of something entirely different from my peers. And that I needed to craft what I had into a set of superpowers that could shield me from the sharp words and messy jokes of fifth graders.

# fabric, wood, paint, and strings (mangum st. 2005)

repetition
sitting on the floor
toner
emails

the words of the black woman writer deities
the hours before usual
new sun
devotion

paper always paper
then thicker paper
pressed black ink
my hands

And I did create a set of superpowers, or at least I thought they were superpowers, to keep myself safe in the tokenization I navigated from my earliest education right through graduate school. But by the time I moved to Durham, North Carolina, to get a PhD in English at Duke in 2004, I felt like I might be outgrowing my shield. And it was the trees, or at least my relationship to paper, that helped me find ways to be present that, if not always safe, were accompanied. The accompaniment of ancestors, the technologies of finding other Black feminists, the feeling of contributing to a multigenerational community. I woke up early and created a Black feminist heaven and used paper to invite other people into it. I thought of myself as practicing in the tradition of post-emancipation Black schoolteachers; I imagined myself in communion with Black women who offered their creativity to generations of learning. I did not know the name Alma Thomas. Yet.

# fabric, wood, paint, and strings (overlook hospital 1982)

*for Pauline McKenzie*

breath
coral
saltwater
sinew

death
mineral
blood
continue

eyelash
cheekbone
pressure
that full head of hair

What is the fabric, what is the wood, what is the paint, what are the strings? Maybe this is what Alma Thomas called "transforming energy."[50] Returning to the scene of my own birth, a C-section in which doctors cut cords prematurely, I can reimagine the materiality of my connection to my mother and to the universe. Questioning what I am made of, I can question what we make and remake collectively. I can make space to notice and to grieve what it means that even before I was learning to be a student or a teacher, institutions averse to Black life were trying to tell me how and when to be born. Threatened by the time my mother needed to bring me here, they were already disciplining the throughline. My mother says that when I was born I had a conehead, shaped by the tools that brought me out instead of the shape of moving through her. And though I am shaped, quite literally, by all of that interference, I am not made of it. My geography is oceanic and unlimited; my beauty school is the abundant wet presence of life.

I wrote dozens of these "fabric, wood, paint, strings" stanzas. And I encourage you to write some too. I think you might learn something about what you are made of. And what you can make. The biggest result of reexamining my education is realizing that there are more subjects for me to study than I can ever name. In fact, the basic questions of puppet formation give me the opportunity to learn something more than the logic of being subject to power. What happens when I take responsibility? When I say, *See that energy? I'm the one who put it there. These are my materials.*

The visionary thinker and activist Grace Lee Boggs theorized that in addition to revolutionaries we need solutionaries, people dedicated to finding solutions to the complex problems that face us as an interconnected mass of life.[51] At the Allied Media Conference in Detroit, Michigan, in 2007, I listened to Boggs say that if our educational systems were just that, intergenerational spaces where we figured out how to solve the problems of water supply, of how to care for one another, of sustainable food systems, we would learn all the math, all the critical thinking, all the history, all the creative writing, all the biology we need at the same time. And what stage have you built? And what story are you acting out? And whom have you conscripted into your drama, tying their hands and feet? If only we could let our need lead our learning instead of reproducing what we think already exists. Alma Thomas knew this, and in her marionette practice she was a teacher of all topics. But most importantly, she offered the practice of supporting bodies and creating new stages. She gave children opportunities to play with connection and light. She asked them to invite the whole community into a story that needed telling. An alternate system created by and for Black children, a respectful use of rope and trees and breath. The pedagogy of a worthy prayer.

# fabric, wood, paint, and strings

## or, material elements of some years of the artist's life

matted hair my grandmothers pulled out in their sleep
trees that held their backs
well mixed watercolor tea
whale intestine

white paper i waxed and blackened with every crayon in the box
popsicle sticks i collected the slow way
the blue of candied teeth
fraying frizzy yarn

flannel
clarinet reed
hypercolor
spiral plugged in phone

dayplanner covers
stacked soles of platform shoes
newspaper ink
flatiron cord

jeans i wore until they fell apart
floors of dorm room nights
printer acrylic t-shirt transfers
ropes that lift windows

*Clown,* c. 1935. Fabric, wood, paint, and strings, 22 × 10 × 3 ¼ in. Columbus Museum, GA, Gift of Miss John Maurice Thomas in memory of her parents, John H. and Amelia W. Cantey Thomas.

glued spines of books
reclaimed church fan handles
blood
cheese

photocopied poems
cheryll's picture frame
markers staining fingers
yard grass

letters of invitation
well maintained forest trails
likes
luggage tags

boarding passes
tea stirrers
honey
the word "yes"

blanket sweatpants
houseplant stems
spice mix
mask loops

most of the fabric is paper
most of the wood is actually wood
most of the paint is edible
most of the string is still here

# fabric, wood, paint, and strings

## or, material elements of some years of the artist's life II

amniotic water
bone of daughter
skin of caul
navel string

mother's kisses
hair and nails
father's heat
bassinet mobile

paradigm of play
side screen door
sugared milk
velcro straps

test scores
leaves
stickers
friendship bracelet lanyards

pleated uniform blue
monkey bar legs
sweat
the word "only"

the written word
afterschool activity
nail polish
a ride home

quotes printed on the wall
fall spring
cranberry juice
and blackness

generations
meetings
blog posts
use

brilliance
podium
publishing
the word "wow"

my love
where we live
vegan chicken broth
asking

the fabric is validation
the wood is what i lean on
the paint is not sustainable
the strings are what i need

# fabric, wood, paint, and strings (highland avenue 1982)

light
skin
milk
fingers

cotton
sleep
kiss
time

heat
arms
soap
laughter

# fabric, wood, paint, and strings (c. 1986)

*for Ariana*

shifting soil
pressed bones
tv screens
distance

smart pretty
first middle
red yellow
summer

sleepover whispers
your strong mouth
stink poetics
mom

# fabric, wood, paint, and strings (plainfield c. 1990)

*for Nisa*

jokes
nick at nite
smirk
and rolling eyes

jamaican food
running upstairs
our hands
our mothers' voices

the position of the sun
the backs of our heads
our different schools
and days

# fabric, wood, paint, strings (duke university fall 2004)

ragtop
attic eaves
lemonade
wireless

shirts of my own design
perkins library tables
stacks of books and printed articles
instrumental tracks

the ubiquitous shawl
seminar sprawl
lack of drawl
every word

# fabric, wood, paint, and strings (durham 2006)

*for ubuntu*

sustainable transformative love
living room furniture
markers on big paper
meetings upon meetings

the parts of myself i was scared to love
stretched over systemic clarity
soaked in black feminist poetry
hung to dry

the world we want to make
whatever art we have
our tears and snot and sweat
our hands

# the art of knowing (what you're made of)

the day time cuts
the strings

your hands
fall to your lap

those loops
drilled in your head
don't lift you up
no more

your eyes
stay open

your lips be
pursed

if you know
who you are
in stillness

who can bind
your soul?

*Woman,* c. 1935. Fabric, wood, paint, and strings, 23 ¾ × 13 × 3 in. Columbus Museum, GA, Gift of Miss John Maurice Thomas in memory of her parents, John H. and Amelia W. Cantey Thomas.

# on children

This is a book inspired by an artist informed by the death of at least one child and accountable to generations of children. And as I write this, all over the world children are dying, like Fannie did, from preventable and treatable diseases, including in my Global North hometown, thanks to a predatory system of "healthcare." As I write this, "man's inhumanity to man" is operating at record rates as computers collaborate with generals to demolish schools and hospitals full of children in Gaza. As I write this, the streets of Alma Thomas's hometown, the U.S. capital, fill again and again with her students, even if they do not know her name, lifting banners and signs and sometimes even puppets in protest of the multiple genocides, in Palestine, Congo, and Sudan, underwritten by the United States' dependency on oil and cobalt.

Those of us involved in the creative practice of insisting on love and solidarity in the face of cruelty and greed are using direct action protest as one visible and auditory way of speaking out. In 1963, after Alma Thomas attended the largest direct action demonstration up to that time, the March on Washington, she had an image she wanted to convey of the massive crowd of people holding signs. She created multiple sketches on canvas board before creating the final painting. In each image we can distinguish the mass of people, faceless and merging into each other from the unreadable white rectangular placards rising behind them, sometimes like an avalanche, sometimes like a breaking wall, sometimes like a boxy cloud of witness. The people could be any of us rising to the moment. The protest signs could say what we need them to say now. The most notable difference in the final version of *March on Washington* is not only its brightness, but the fact that there is drastically more sky. Significantly more visible earth. When you look at the final piece in contrast to the sketches, the increased space of blue behind the rows of signs and the blue yellow green ground from which the brighter, more numerous protesting figures emerge make it seem like the increased brightness comes not only from Thomas's choice to use the most vibrant paint for the actual painting, but also from the sun herself. The people don't only stand and march, they bloom into possibilities we are still drawing strength from. And now when the sun shines on us gathered chanting in our city center as we grieve together, holding our cardboard visions up higher than we can actually reach, I say, thank you, Alma.

Maya Freelon, an artist born and raised in Durham, North Carolina, who also taught for a time in the DC public schools, told me Alma Thomas is a primary influence on her work. Her large-scale works use water to transform the colorful tissue paper used in a school art classroom into monumental three-dimensional paper quilts that have filled museums, galleries, and public spaces all over the world, shifting airy white institutions into landscapes of possibility. The question of where the sky ends or begins floats around us. Where colors bleed, perception transforms.

I recently attended *Whippersnappers,* an installation and ceremony Freelon cultivated during her time in DC as a Library of Congress artist-in-residence researching photographs of enslaved children. This time Freelon decided to take over a place of thick air and heavy history, an unwhitewashable context. The *Whippersnappers* installation inhabits Stagville, a massive historic plantation that has shaped the lives of everyone in our shared hometown of Durham. Under Freelon's transformation, the "big house" at Stagville spills over with images of the energy of Black children. Black children in contemplation. Black children in confrontation. Black children in the midst of joy and play. All of these bright ghost children straining against the limits of chattel slavery and the comfort of the enslaving family who lived in this home, a family at the base of the national tobacco industry, whose unremunerated profits from the enslaved labor and the sale, use, and abuse of these children continue to accrue with interest, providing generations of beneficiaries with enough money to become major investors in contemporary art. The "great barn" on the plantation, vibrationally full with a massive paper quilt and a sound installation created by Dr. Allie Martin and her Black Sound Lab, features the voice of Martin's mother singing and the wind over her grandmother's grave, in honor of her ancestors who experienced slavery in this region.

Freelon, a mother of three children, including a child named Wonderful who lived only for a few moments after birth, created a ceremony to honor child ancestors bound by a system of abject dehumanization. It should not be possible to hold the reality of childhood and the violence of slavery, the reality of childhood and the cruelty of apartheid, the reality of childhood and the evil of genocide, in the same breath at the same moment. And yet, we live in a world shaped by these contradictions. As you read this, unless by the miracle of our transformation we have already won the dignity our children deserve, the unimaginable is routine. At Stagville, around the fire outside the dwelling that the enslaved ancestors built for themselves, Maya and her mother, the cherished jazz singer Nnenna Freelon, facilitated a ceremony where we spoke love over the archival names of children who had been enslaved. We embarrassed, humbled, and renewed ourselves playing children's games that came out of their tradition of resistance. We made our voices and our bodies into homes for the lessons they still need to teach us.

And I thought about how proud Alma Thomas might be to know that she inspires an artist such as Maya Freelon who understands that the creativity of children exists and must be honored. Alma Thomas's work was not to feed the children (though she did train them to make woodcut print menus), not directly to house and clothe the children (though she did participate in her church's multiple charitable ministries and founded some), and not to only enrich the minds of the children with facts (though she was indeed on the Negro History Week committee every year). Her focus was on the creative possibility of their aliveness in form. She provided imaginative resources and served their openness to the beautiful.

And then I went home. And the next day came, and children in Gaza died while trying to access water and food. And children of the Congo died or were orphaned, or were forced to become child soldiers. And the children and youth of Sudan fell in an ongoing coup while the world turned its back. What is the bridge between the work Alma Thomas guides me to do to study and free my younger self, to become a sister to possibility beyond pragmatism—and my urgent need to respond to man's inhumanity to children? How can I focus without betraying my duty and my love? I began a new daily practice at first light. Instead of looking at Alma's paintings and artifacts, I researched names of children, seeking the prayer I needed to pray over the world that sacrificed them. Because the name of every child is a prayer.

Often I failed. The names of children who have died may or may not be available. Their families may be holding those prayers close. The deaths may be too numerous and sudden for proper memorialization or even identification. The children facing death by other names may have their names redacted to protect them from further harm. And I want you to live more than I want to have access to your name for my poem. The poems came different than I expected them to come. The colors bled. I started with the names of siblings in one Gazan family killed by an Israeli air strike while their mother worked in a hospital tending other bombed children. I wrote of the names a journalist invented to talk about the child survivors in a Congolese orphanage. The pseudonyms of the rape survivors in the group home in Haiti. The nine-year-old little girl in the United States of America forced to carry a pregnancy from the rape she survived, due to anti-abortion laws in her state that may become national. I could only call her by her small number of years. I wrote new prayers for the children in my own life. I wrote poems to the children I began to see in the faces of the adults around me. I have to trouble the distance between earth and sky. I have to listen. Sister is not a responsibility that ends.

The poems of that process are mostly private. I write them in my journal, not on this computer. In teaching myself about the names, the misnaming, the unnameable, I am learning humility. As I learned on the day I read the Surah of Luqman in the Koran in honor of little Luqman lost in rubble:

> If all the trees on earth were pens and the ocean were ink refilled
> by seven other oceans the words of Allah would not be exhausted.[52]

There is more.

There is more to say, there is more to do, there is more than this charade of disconnection. There is more than the destructive system I am complicit with in every transaction, every drive. There is more. Dedication to the creativity of children in a world structured to sacrifice the vulnerable again and again takes heart, imagination, persistence, strength. A way to come back. Again. Again.

# red impressions

# alma's prayer

i came to make flowers out of broken earth
shake some sweetness out this place
god you sent me to georgia
where i learned my love was red

i came to make vases out of broken faces
some sense out of this mess
you sent me just in time
to see tree limbs weighed down with blood

i came to make beauty out of caked up hate
my duty to a world of spite
most freeing thing about it?
no way i could do right

i came to make oceans out of fields of grass
offer salt to the weeping ground
attuned to hear love in the saddest sound
here i am lord. here i am.

*Grassy Melodic Chant,* 1976. Acrylic on canvas, 46 × 36 in. Smithsonian American Art Museum, Washington, DC.

# a red blues for alma

i glue my mosaic to the world of skin
all my sacred broken pieces to the smooth world of sin

blood my vitamins earth my kin
fix all my sacred longings to the racist world i'm in

my morning my noonday my impulse to begin
every jagged inch of knowing 'bout the place i been

strawberries, peaches, cough syrup, gin
i smear my liquid memories. brush and start again

my royal bloodline my exiled swim
i sing a torn libretto steady in the blue-eyed din

mustard seed belief red sea open and thin
the songs of 7 million in a dented tin

cloudless sky and fertilizer blend
i'd give all my burning memoirs for a peaceful when

trafficked road open glen
eventually the shattered sister wins

*Nature's Red Impressions,* 1968. Acrylic on canvas, 48 × 50 in. GW Collection, courtesy of the Luther W. Brady Art Gallery, George Washington University, Washington, DC.

# what alma sang while she painted rock and roll

one part kool-aid
one part hibiscus

baby mix my blood
break my cells

free me into
immunity and air

all those scraps of you
that flow through me

i'll leave them everywhere

steal my lipstick
write my story
spell my mouth with lies

(every time a woman wears red
a grown man somewhere
cries)

shuffle my spread
into sixes and sevens
press off all my nails
red clay girls like me
got stories

oh these hands
have tales

*Red Azaleas Singing and Dancing to Rock and Roll Music,* 1976. Acrylic on three canvases, 73 ¾ × 158 ½ in. (overall). Smithsonian American Art Museum, Washington, DC.

# aside

i used to wonder if the shadows knew something
they weren't telling me
and if i could just be quieter
i would hear what they whispered to each other

turns out i could
   in time i did
that's right
                                        i can

*Untitled* (*Study for Fiery Sunset*), c. 1973. Acrylic on paper, 5 ¼ × 6 in. James E. Hall and Kelli Hall.

# what god told alma

this is what i used
to make a riot
a rainbow
a coral reef
a tesseract

this is a portrait
of the first moment
of the universe

or is it the last

behold
a planet
covered in its
black oil blood

blooming blooming
like everybody
else.

*Untitled,* undated. Acrylic and watercolor on paper, 22 × 28 in. Private collection.

# organ

i am small
and the world is red
and the sound is tall
and i bow my head

and the world is red
and the habits white
and i bow my head
in the blessed light

and the things we do
without knowing why
in the blessed light
of the falling sky

without knowing who
we were born to be
when the falling sky
set our breathing free

we were born to be
while the largest sound
sets our breathing free
in the smallest round.

*Saint Cecilia at the Organ* (*Etude in Brown*), 1962. Oil on linen, 44 × 28 in. Christian Levett Collection.

# ochre dream

they circle
humming
hands outstretched
the fingers of their left hands
meeting in the middle
the nails of their right hands
red from the walls of my womb

they fall
singing
red into fabric
print their map
where i can see it
when i wash out
the blood cloth
baptize my clay feet
in memory

the first cave paintings
turned rock into blood

the last billionaires
point their shuttles
to mars

my mothers are painting me
ochre as sky
flying home
from the inside
out

*Mars Dust,* 1972. Acrylic on canvas, 69 ¼ × 57 ⅛ in. Whitney Museum of American Art, New York.

# what the wise ones said

all of us women
held in pieces by our clothes
standing on the cobbled gravestones
of our names

and the light pink world around us
a shattered sunrise shaded
what we did to our eyes
looking for stars

we are blood we are rain
we are gold          bow before us
standing tight and close
against the cold

once upon a time
there was a drum

it woke us

once upon a time
there was a barn

we found it

once upon a time
there was a night

we broke it
with our gifts

*Three Wise Men,* 1966. Acrylic on canvas, 36 ½ × 23 ½ in. Harmon and Harriet Kelley Foundation for the Arts, San Antonio.

# alma speaks of loss

once upon a time there was a world
in wolf's clothing
a monster
eating my beautiful world

or

when i realized
that we would not get
not even one flower
out the garden
not even one stem of grass
to keep and take with us
when they ran us off our red clay land
i learned something about color
that i refuse
to now abide

*Untitled,* c. 1966. Watercolor on paper, 9 ½ × 12 in. James E. Hall and Kelli Hall.

# inventory

i remember patch of dirt
i remember spill
i remember open hand
surprised face
chill

i remember smudge of breath
i remember soot
i remember root down
uproot

i remember bare feet
in the backyard grass
i remember tight shoes
haters walking past

i remember oil spill
i remember flight
i remember no moon
  rocket light

i remember hibiscus
all falling apart
catastrophe so common
it's art

*Untitled,* 1960s. Watercolor on paper, 5 ¼ × 8 in. Columbus Museum, GA, Gift of Miss John Maurice Thomas in memory of her parents, John H. and Amelia W. Cantey Thomas.

# oya in autumn

from the crowd the people scatter
the people fall
the people dance

in the fall
we become light
we become red yellow and brown
the air picks us up to dance
oh yes to dance

in the dance we become
fallen
we be folly
we be fellow fallow fools

in the fellowship
we lose it
we learn what
we never needed
let it leave

in the loss
we let our backs go
watch our shoes slip
lose the only bones
we know

in the knowing
we are naked
we are losing

*Wind Tossing Late Autumn Leaves,* 1976. Acrylic on canvas, 72 × 52 in. New Jersey State Museum Collection, Trenton.

who to be
and what to do

in the being
we are knowing
what we not

in the unknot
we are loose
we are loose

free of tree
free of noose
free of use

# every age

My strategy of self-defense is to transform pain into meaning.

—Adrian Piper

The closest the conceptual artist Adrian Piper comes to anything resembling an Alma Thomas color painting has neither color, nor paint. In 1968, at the height of Thomas's active color painting practice, Piper constructed an artist's book called *Here and Now,* a cardboard portfolio with sixty-four loose-leaf pages with grids of sixty-four spaces on each page. With this work, which also includes instructions for the multiple ways to arrange the loose-leaf pages, she created a physical manifestation of her idea of the "indexical present." Each intersecting line marks a point of presence. The only job of the work is to notify the viewer where "here" is. For example, one square contains the text "Here: the square area in the third row from the top, fourth from the right side," which is its exact location on the page.[53] Here is here. Black lines. White space. Each page resembles Alma Thomas's dashed lines of color almost in inverse. Where every single one of Thomas's painterly marks is unique though related to every other mark, Piper's grid seeks to emulate the supposed uniformity of time. The exactness of place. The materiality of presence and the describability of its particularity. Where Thomas's paintings radiate with what Richard Powell calls "high key color techniques," Piper's grids do not even require gray scale for reproduction.[54]

This is all as it should be. Because the project of Adrian Piper is not the project of Alma Thomas. Contrast Adrian Piper's disruptive performance art, cross-dressing and passing across racial and gendered lines or riding public transportation drenched in foul-smelling liquid, to Thomas's work to gain her students dignified access to previously all-white art galleries in Washington, DC. Contrast Piper's work to unsettle racial and gender perception with Alma Thomas's work to facilitate Negro History Week pageants about African excellence at Shaw Junior High School. The project of Alma Thomas is not the project of Adrian Piper. And how could it be? That we know of, Thomas and Piper do not seem to have engaged each other's work or met or collaborated in any way. There is no meeting point on the grid where they share the same time, the same place, the indexical present that Piper describes as "What is going on in this minute between you and me."[55]

But what if there was?

Alma Thomas's description of her work as the view of one flying above and Adrian Piper's recurrent dreams of flying lead me to bring Piper up here. Piper says, "It's the view from an airplane on a cloudless day, but without windows, cabin or seat-belt."[56] And her definition of abstraction as flying and flight, or the "freedom to imagine the possible and transport oneself into it; freedom to survey the real as a resource for embodying the possible," has left me with a recurrent fantasy of the two artists meeting.[57]

It would be an energizing but tense meeting point. Their work side by side might feel full and dizzying, pulling one back and forth like the transformative meeting points between the deep-blue and bright-orange colors in Alma Thomas's *Fiery Sunset.* It might feel disorienting and generatively unsafe, like encountering Piper enacting her embodied disruptions of what she calls xenophobia on public transportation or a city street. Piper explains, "My work springs from a belief that we are transformed—and occasionally reformed—by immediate experience, independently of our abstract evaluations of it and despite our attempts to resist it."[58] The indexical present for Piper is "not something that is full of external associations, suppositions, preconceptions."[59]

Alma Thomas describes her work as something like "abstract evaluation." She says, "Art is inevitably the expression of external conditions, modified though they be by the genius and personality of the artist."[60]

But this is Piper's protest; she seeks to destroy the inevitability of what she calls "xenophobia," which she means to include every oppressive relation based on perceived difference, by insisting that now is now. Meet me here, she insists, in *this* moment.

Or at least that's what she insisted half a century ago. Would Piper have a problem with the current version of me referencing a mid-twentieth-century version of her descriptions of her work? Maybe not. Confronted with what she perceived to be constant misinterpretations of her work within an oppressive arts industry, she admitted, "I comfort myself with the thought that future generations of viewers for whom the problems of racism and xenophobia will be less pressing and threatening will surely provide the positive aesthetic evaluations I would like."[61]

I don't think that racism and xenophobia are "less pressing" problems for my generation, though they manifest in different forms from what Piper experienced in the mid- to late twentieth century, and even more so what Thomas experienced from the nineteenth century through the twentieth century. But maybe Piper would find it appropriate that I find it impossible to talk about my poetic indexes of Thomas's color fields and my own practice of presence without referencing her work on the indexical present.

The indexes themselves? You'll see. They are aggressively associative, abstracted attempts at resistance, interdependent with everything in my imagined universe.

The decolonial Antiguan-American writer Jamaica Kincaid's narrative *See Now Then* refuses to honor a mutually exclusive binary between "here and now" and "then and there" because, as she insisted recently to a curious and confused gathering of readers at the Seattle Public Library,

> the orderliness of what happened is only interesting to the people who caused it to happen but to the victims of it, it's of no use, and it doesn't at all capture the wretchedness and the wreckage and the horror. The only thing that can contain it is just writing. And the categories, fiction, non-fiction are not important, these categories inhibit the truth, for certain of us they are of no use, they are of no use to what needs to be said.[62]

My teacher the Trinidadian transnational Black feminist M. Jacqui Alexander argues for this refusal of binaries and criticality of the reproductive uses of time and space as a key to decolonial possibility, or what she calls "a map outside the mandate for conquest."[63] The map of the mandate for conquest places the West as here and now, or modern, and the colonized world as "then and there," and this doesn't only obscure the complexity of reality: "Time and distance are ineluctably circumscribed," and conscripted into the continued reproduction of the conditions of coloniality.[64] So, towards a reckoning with that reality and the creation of something else, Kincaid and Alexander insist it is all here and there. It is then now.

Now then, Kincaid sets about saying what needs to be said, first to herself and then eventually to a puzzled world full of reviewers who must find something to say about the new work of such a prominent literary figure, and who in most cases waste their time trying to parse the exact line between fiction and nonfiction. The reviewers Kincaid complains about want to find out through internet research how much the family of the novel who lives in New England, like Kincaid's family, actually *is* Kincaid's living family. This is precisely beside the point.

For the readers, for the public, for the people at the public library in Seattle, Kincaid explains that she is engaged in a project about time.

> The main character, the greatest character in the novel is the thing we call time and it refers to the time that they're in which is the present which would be now and then would be their past or their future. But it also refers a lot to geologic time which is incomprehensible really at least to my imagination. And so it's all bound up in moments. It's sort of an attempt on my part to make all of existence into one moment. Always now. Always now. It is also an attempt of mine to understand the thing we call time which is incomprehensible and must be one of those things called "social constructs." Time is indifferent to whether we can measure it or not.[65]

And then she warns the audience before she begins to read, "You will feel a bit at sea."[66]

And, as always, *See Now Then* is, like Kincaid's other works, oceanic, recursive, it explores the possibility of always now, or the presence of everything, a presence so suffused with context it requires repetition and mythology. It is aggressively associative. The family lives in "the Shirley Jackson house," a fact that does not simply set the scene but invokes Jackson, author of haunted family dramas, every time the house is mentioned. The names of the family members, Mrs. and Mr. Sweet and the lovely Persephone and the young Heracles, must carry their modifiers ("sweet," "lovely," "young") every time they are referenced by the unreliable narrator ("so unreliable," in Kincaid's public evaluation), Mrs. Sweet herself.[67]

We learn about the main character, the greatest character, time, through the contradiction of the narrative. Not the crisis of the narrative, because that would be a plot point, but the ongoing contradiction of the fact that the family Mrs. Sweet creates, her husband, daughter, and son, resent the family she keeps writing about in the room next to the kitchen, her melancholic relationship to her larger than life, epic, haunting parents. Especially her mother.

I will remind you that the life of Jamaica Kincaid, a tall pre-punk iconoclast who dyed her hair orange to make herself stand out even more as a young au pair turned writer in New York City, does not share much with the life of Alma Thomas, though Kincaid may have lived in New York during Alma's exhibition at the Whitney. And also the life of Jamaica Kincaid is not the life of *See Now Then*'s Mrs. Sweet, who works in and near her kitchen. Jamaica Kincaid does not live in the home of a famous woman writer. She did raise her family across the street from the house where Shirley Jackson wrote and died. And sometimes one paints the light that comes in through the window.

And yet, the most direct and visible manifestation of the grudge Mrs. Sweet's husband and children have towards her comes directly into Alma Thomas's purview. They resent her relationship to color. They abhor what she does with paint. They pray for the death and destruction of the flowers in her garden.

Somewhere in the then, Mr. Sweet had loved Mrs. Sweet and "the way she could exaggerate, so that if she saw ten tulips in a vase, she would say she saw ten thousand daffodils at a glance, tossing their heads in a sprightly dance; she would sometimes put a rainbow in the sky, just because it was a beautiful day but she thought it should be more so and a rainbow would be just the thing." But in the now, that then is "revolting to Mr. Sweet, for a kitchen counter should be white or marble or just plain wood but Mrs. Sweet would go out of her way to find such an abomination, yellow Formica, to cover the counter and then she would paint the wall in the kitchen those Caribbean colors: mango, pineapple, not peaches and nectarine."[68]

So intrusive is Mrs. Sweet's abundant relationship to color that Mr. Sweet breaks into a botanical litany while celebrating with the children "as if addressing an audience" that "all the tulips your mother planted last autumn were eaten by the deer, a deer with six antlers, a clever old deer with good and malicious taste; the deer came and ate them all, just as they were about to bloom, just as they had reached that point in budding before bursting into bloom, the deer came and ate them."[69] He goes on (possibly only in the mind of Mrs. Sweet) to name all eighteen specific varieties of tulips that Mrs. Sweet had planted, "And the two children burst into applause and clapped their hands and raised their glasses of milk into the air."[70] And so after Mrs. Sweet, transplanted from the Caribbean, waits all winter for her flowers to bloom, whiteness prevails.

Whiteness prevails through the form of the heterosexual family within which Mrs. Sweet's difference will never be integrated, because the same logics of the heterosexual family myth that Kincaid plays with stunningly in the text are what reproduce the colonial exclusion. And the contradiction of Mrs. Sweet's predicament, in which her husband justifies cheating and divorce because of her retention of her own there, and her ongoing then, her failure to sacrifice the then and there to the here and now, is explained as a failure at marriage. As Jacqui Alexander has theorized, "heterosexualization is one of the processes through which globalization is aligned."[71] In *See Now Then* we get a glimpse of how this connection between the individual's incommensurability into the heterosexual marriage form and the imposition of the scale of the nation mirror each other.

Kincaid tells us all of this using her consistent technique, the long sentence, the breathless persistence, the inclusion of more and more until the page is so full that you do see the patterns, the ruptures of white. Does that look familiar?

Maybe it is the case that for Mrs. Sweet the world is a living color field where this time is connected to all time, and her husband and children attempt to fix life in the here and now. Where these same children fed by Mrs. Sweet's elaborate meals and clothed in the handiwork of her tangible love conclude that she must not love them at all because she is late picking them up from school today, because of her infernal tendency to get lost in the practice of writing. Maybe Mrs. Sweet knows what Alma Thomas knows, that color is one of the secrets of transcending linear time and space.

Sometimes people learn something about who they are by viewing my work. For me this is proof of success.

—Adrian Piper

I am learning something about myself.

My selves.

I believe in portals. I believe that every mark of color in Alma Thomas's color paintings is a portal, just like every flower holds worlds of possibility that beckon me to look closer and closer again. Color is relational, and Alma Thomas studied the associative, psychological, and physiological impact of colors. As I engage Thomas's paintings I am confronted with every age of myself, my fiction-nonfiction memories, the run-on sentences I am running away from, but I reconfront them in a blooming heaven. A space abundant enough that I can offer every age of myself something, a sweetness, a hand, a word she needed to hear or say, a visceral remaking of the world. And what if I tried to catalog all the places I went, color by color? That is the basic exercise of the Color Indexes that follow.

And my imperative is the combined imperative of everyone I have mentioned here. My imperative is to be present. My condition is the always now. My insistence is to liberate everyone I ever was from the colonial and heterosexist stories I believed about myself.

But don't try to glean my biography from the indexes below, because it is no longer about me. It is about what meets us in the moment of your reading. Where it takes you. What it brings back. Here is not here. Then is not finished. And yet, despite everything, I am with you.

Jacqui uses the concept of palimpsestic time layered over itself, much like Kincaid's scaffold of a diasporic here and there, throughout her book *Pedagogies of Crossing,* but then at the end of the book she exceeds it. Kind of like what happens to me at some point in each of these poems. She confesses:

> Time as metaphysical is not disciplined by neat compartmentalizations of finance, the clock, the "here and now" and the "then and there," nor is it even governed by the "here and there" of our model of palimpsesis. Time transforms and much like the serpent, that ancient figure of metamorphosis, returns to provoke the encounter with the lost double that memory makes impossible to forget.[72]

All our lost doubles (Trinidadian pun intended). All my lost doubles. Or as the Afro-Caribbean Lesbian Warrior Poet Audre Lorde would say in her poem "Call," for the deity Aida Wedo, all the versions of ourselves "stolen out of (y)our name(s) . . . whose faces have been forgotten."[73]

Here is my rainbow serpent, a ceremony of reclamation, indexes of possible encounters for every age of us.

# blue data

# arrival

in the beginning there was the ocean and the ocean was broken and the ocean breathed itself back together like confetti on a sticky party floor in the first hours of the new year in a cosmic neighborhood bar. and under the layers of breathing there was a sulfur world a seep a deep chemical thinking and the geniuses already adapting invented tongues and inner lips and blood and other salts to pull the moon back from wherever she was going. and under that the hardened thoughts of planets brittle round the whispers of the ones who flew apart back into stars the temperature charts of dust the snow of timelessness. and inside all that the sun and outside all that the sun and around the sun the first and lasting homework. the sweetest softest gold to glint the memory of sky the flaking of an atmosphere into its jazz components into its mountain echoed grass-seed into its triple chorus blues. she used her teeth to tear the sound back into gravity her dress of kelp the tangled clock legs of the universe. her chlorophyll a prayer to let go all her petty thoughts her crown of roundest stones smoothing her days away a million at a time. every afternoon when ground crashed in to build volcanoes she soothed herself with wildflower explosions and listened for the whisper of a violet meeting wind while lava slowed itself to granite in her name. and yet once there was blood there was time. once there was blood there was forward. once there was blood there was a place for salt to live and sculpt itself into a dream bomb threaded with grass and unspat futures. once there was blood there was history and rust. but in the beginning there was only space and breathing. in the beginning there was only sweat and ice. in the beginning there was shell and shape and round was not an aspiration or reminder. and she wore sharp sea urchin earrings so you'd listen. she wore pearls to get your gut to know her name. she wore baleen bellbottoms sewn with coral fans and just like that sargassoed all your plans. immediately cathedraled your lagoon. and instantly you couldn't breathe inside her. and all at once your fate required lungs. your hands required spoons.

*Light Blue Nursery,* 1968. Acrylic on canvas, 49 × 47 ⅞ in. Smithsonian American Art Museum, Washington, DC, Gift of the artist.

# model

first they made me butter
and i slid down into the world
in search of a pancake to call
home

then they made me salt
and i drowned in a million pieces
sweat myself into ocean
haven't stopped crying
yet

when they made me sugar
i broke their teeth with smiling
i curried their blood with thickness
i took them limb by limb

at last they made me cotton
i took in every drop
thickened fat into my destiny
finally learned
to swim

*Bust of a Young Girl,* 1923. Plaster, 13 × 9 × 5 in. Columbus Museum, GA, Gift of Miss John Maurice Thomas in memory of her parents, John H. and Amelia W. Cantey Thomas.

# may you have

a day bright enough
all nourishing vitamins
loving foods
generations that sing with you
clean air for every breath

a love
that gives you space
to live
your complex dark

a yes
that lets you bleed
beyond the torn edge
of the world

*Spectrum,* 1972/76. Acrylic on paper, 22 × 30 in. Private collection.

# transmission

first rule of the ocean
protect the light at the core
first rule of the ocean
remember who invented birth

second statement from the ocean
i am what i hold i am what i hide
second statement from the ocean
i am transforming deep and wide
second statement from the ocean
you know my salt you know my tears
second statement from the ocean
you can never measure my age in years

third missive from the light
before reflection before sight
third missive from the light
my broken journey brief and bright
third missive from the light
my elemental glimmer stays
third missive from the light
for cosmic days through waves and rays
it stays it stays it stays it stays

fourth testament of the bones
we kept the light we held inside
fourth testament of the bones
we fed the multitudes and tides
fourth testament of the bones
an orb of calcium and grief
fourth testament of the bones
shell of protection and relief

*Light Flash,* 1974. Acrylic on paper, 22 ½ × 30 in. Susan Kaim Talley and Bascom D. Talley III.

fifth inscription in the deep
you know the coral never sleeps
keeps breathing intergenerational reef
her structure death her tenant's teeth
she laughs at every builder's dream
and writes her waking name on earth
again

sixth offering from the sky
i am where i am why
i am falling
sixth offering from the sky
i am lie i am truth
i am calling
sixth offering from the sky
i am full i am free
i am free

seventh answer from the dead
we want our references to come
in living prayers
seventh answer from the dead
we want your days layered in fathoms
not in stairs
seventh answer from the dead
we heard your question
this is what we want
instead

# origin story

in the beginning there was the moon
orbiting around nothing
gravitationally free
rock beyond relation

in the beginning there was you
no need of me
not even black dust
in your imagination

in the sky there was a breath
that no one heard
it was a word
we still outliving

and when matter opened
full of light
the color offered
beautiful night

and when ocean let
herself be round
that was the sound
i found you

*Genesis,* 1966. Watercolor on paper, 21 ½ × 29 ½ in. D. Steven Sharp Collection.

# blue

*for Clyde Gumbs*

I

the way stripes curve
around the globe of your shoulder
world in my hands

rose glow around the universe
your skin metabolizing me into kin
you becoming something else
in my blurry eyes

my baby hair
your atmosphere

II

love will be
a tennis ball
a classic sneaker
a bounce against sidewalk
a shield in your teeth
protecting me from the memory
of the philadelphia police
harassing you
on the way to play basketball
and again on the way back
to school

III

anything can become armor
white car
blue collar
shoelace
cheekbone
that ocean
starting up
in your eyes

IV

strap of your gym bag
accent of your shoe
stripe on your shoulder
underside of your collar
smurfs on the tv
and you

V

best chance
is the neon light
the open court
the black
against our brown

best strategy?
smile like broad daylight
hope they can see

VI

but even in the light
the blue of your face
blue in the face from explaining
blue moon of standing alone
once in a blue moon
your spirit glints through
all the grime of this

VII

under your skin
is a red world
a flame
the way they get
under your skin
only feeds it

under your skin
is a sun reaching
from its corner of the universe
to cradle you
in gold

*Snoopy Sees a Sunrise,* 1970. Acrylic on canvas, 48 × 48 in. National Air and Space Museum, Washington, DC.

# on being blue I

*for Karl Osborne*

i learned to call you from underneath
and the signal went up in all directions
i learned the ocean had hallways
where a sound could get lost

and the signal went up in all directions
and i sunk ever further
where a sound could get lost
this was my hiding place

and i sunk ever further
surrendered to depth
this was my hiding place
this was my peace

surrendered to depth
i forgot my name
this was my peace
in blue

i forgot my name
in the hallways of the sea
in blue
i learned how to call you

Karl Osborne took Audre Lorde's class on systemic racism at John Jay College while working as an NYPD officer. In one of his papers for the class, he processed the racism he experienced from white NYPD colleagues and grieved the deaths of his Black colleagues who were killed on the job by their own white colleagues. He was told to believe in "blue" solidarity among police, but he wrote: "There is little to make a black officer feel blue; other than sadness." Audre Lorde Papers, Spelman College, Atlanta, box 82, folder 2.

*Untitled,* 1977. Acrylic on paper, 22 × 30 in. National Gallery of Art, Washington, DC, promised gift from a private collection.

# on being blue II

*for Detective Capers and Patrolman Wright*
*(two of the Black NYPD officers shot and killed*
*by white NYPD officers in the 1970s)*

i am the sea monster
press my hands
into waves
they become sharks
and sinking ships

and this is why i'm blue
and this is why i'm strong
and this is why you don't see me
at night

red lights
warn in whispers
from my breast
and both my knees

i brace myself
against the sea
as if
it's ground
as if i'm free

as if there's any solid earth
for me

*Blue Night* (*At Sea*), 1959. Oil on canvas, 40 × 30 ⅛ in. Columbus Museum, GA, Gift of Miss John Maurice Thomas in memory of her parents, John H. and Amelia W. Cantey Thomas and her sister Alma Woodsey Thomas.

# blue

this is how i want you to love me
blue over blue over blue
wet til the paper buckles
dark so the owls come out

blue

and at the edge a mountain
that knows no country
respects no borders
don’t care when i forget
my own name

your love so jangles my blood
now the sunrise be sudden

*Untitled* (from *Atmospheric Effects*), 1970. Watercolor on paper, 20 × 30 in. D. Steven Sharp Collection.

# new galaxy

everything was breaking. everyone was blue. everyone was not. telling each other how cerulean. how ocean. how back of humpback. how buried sapphire. how top lip kool-aid. how cornflower. how checkered tablecloth. how bottom of sarah vaughan's voice they actually felt.

they actually felt. for the edges of blue. and they found early morning. they found their own mothers singing. they found surprised and cataracted blinking. they found lake of drowned marble round. they found waiting sky to fall into.

to fall into sun. blue has to run. away from itself into dawn. they found bunny and fawn. they found ice and dew. they found me. they found you. offered us up to sunrise.

and if you could have seen it. that blink you blinked right then.

once i saw it. blue was never broke again.

*New Galaxy,* 1970. Acrylic on canvas, 54 × 54 in. Tampa Museum of Art.

spect

# a morning prayer

god be a clementine in my mouth. sweetness in my days. open my heart like sunshine opens morning. free as clover. may my steps spring solid into lusher memories. water. sky. may the faces of my ancestors be what they are. sunflower, supernova, flame. may today be a day so filled with miracles they call it tomorrow. like summer on the top of the world. irrigate me god with blessings for anyone and everyone. confetti my spirit. this burst of joy. forever amen.

*Lunar Rendezvous—Circle of Flowers*, 1969. Acrylic on canvas, 50 × 48 in. Crystal Bridges Museum of American Art, Bentonville, AR.

# portrait

first glasses
violet
salt streaked
tricycle
basket
flowers
blurred
by bees
past
swingset
rising
falling
sweet
and broken
blood
and wrist
  bone
softer
than earth

the rain
remembers
dance recital
eyes of
mamas
blurred
mascara
be black
salt streak
memory
body long
and stretched
to arabesque
pinkskin
tights
to thin
brown arms
extend
further
and further
  out

the grasslit
puffy
weekend face
where air
turns to
crust in your
eye
crust of earth
tastes like
lawnmower
exhale
daddy's
green
portrait
of don't
grass the air
with edges
that your
daughters
cannot
breathe

and leave
the silver
striped car
too many
adidas t-shirts
the sunrise
bloody
in your
absent
way to school
fool
the mountains
roller skate
the steep
summit grade
winding
motionsick
elementary
too late

to dream
of never
sleeping
dream of
robots
dream of
strawberry
darryl
horses
plastic
stables
  rainbow
hair
dollface futures
cartoon songs
the house
is a boat
asphalt
an ocean
carpet sea

match your
clothes
to the idea
of color
every purple
all at once
that every
color come
to find itself
on brown
suggest
infinity
your brave
and quiet
answer
to only
no shade
of lonely
on your
day

away
the land
forever sky
remember
flood and
use your
eyes
to erase
history
the house
is a boat
the bunkbed
a boat too
the girl
motionsick
on land
cannot see
further
than her
hand

shoelaces
zipper
ballet bag
friendship
bracelet
thread
scotch tape
bleachers
of crayons
paper thick
with waxing
over and over
until
  everything
become
black
and black
reveals her
riot purple
sheen

if frosting
housepaint
gingerbread
piping
hot latkes
drunk
dreidels
ways to
cut your
brown
construction
paper hand
to leaf
to never
soft enough
to leave
the childish
lie
i don't like
chocolate

tang is not
enough
our kool-aid
bright
and thick
with cans
of frozen
orange juice
gingerale
and redding
time and
paneled walls
wooden
table wooden
spoon
tan plastic
pitcher
sweetie
smile

*Untitled,* c. 1968. Watercolor on paper, 8 × 10 ½ in. Columbus Museum, GA, Gift of Miss John Maurice Thomas in memory of her parents and her sister.

# hypothetical

start
with brown skin
black eyelashes
open brown eyes
the black hair
of sunday morning

the asphalt awake as tread
the unassuming driveway sky

loop violets
through our baby earholes
easter morning god
remembers small places

throw open the windows

the pink blood of jesus
blooms every year on time
for the easter morning
family photo

perennial open heart
sisters raised to the sound of
  stevie
we too want to come back
as flowers

the photographer's genius
turns you towards the sun
lights your face
with time itself

ask your clothes to do
what azaleas do already
call all the buzzing life
to look
land
light

gentle crusade
across your neck

cultivate the thickness
of your leaving
so sunlight still streams through

take off your glasses
said our mother to our father
so i can swim
in your big brown eyes

the better to drown
the better to fly
the better to inform
my recharting of the sky

daddy nearsighted as all
get out
let light bounce break
into his face

until he could see this future
place of prismed eyes
and dappled grace

*Azaleas Sway with the Breeze,* 1969. Acrylic and graphite on canvas, 72 × 52 in. Michael Rosenfeld Gallery, New York.

a 1970s dream sequence
transition

for a couple
weeks out of every
year the tiny rhododendrons
are the backdrop

for all of us
pink shirted lightskinned smiling
men
lace-socked leather patent
kids
brother in arms

facing the cars
the swarms of the swingset
facing the harms
the reach the not yet

held between window house
and the small road out
the shrub if left untamed
would have renamed
reclaimed the path

the wrath of deciduous might
in an abundance of light
take over
tall enough conspiracy of short
trees flooding the gray out

what if the branches
brambling and bold
bright and not apologizing
lived loud enough to keep him

what if we grew up in a jungle
of easters
our rolled away stones
showing up
like us
in threes

what if the unlandscaped yard
locked around us
faithful as kodak
in a vinegar solution

take off my glasses
and i can see us there
eating flowers for breakfast
pale in our trust

eyes black with hunger
remembering sun

# index for failing at not loving you

kool-aid kool-aid still drinking the kool-aid
bluelipped back stroke still missing the sea
grass-stained drag out leave it in the clearing
your love is such a mystery to me

olive glasses still red in the middle
sunshine sunshade still bleaching the road
tangerine path to smeared remnants of dogsick
rum punch revelation code

sapphire wedding ring promises adventure
emerald street signs leading you astray
trees been made of truth you are ignoring
who told you who told you you should stay

seaglass backpack carry all the summer
bright skin lost kin lost
tortoiseshell accents shine upon your hiding
blue the reason always green the cost

i thought i saw the footsteps of a gorgeous dripping dragon
i thought i heard you screaming at the bottom of the pool
i knew my knees as surfaces where rubies made their comeback
before during between and after school

and to the degree that your hands are darker than your face
and at the point where your palms disclaim your joints
that's the extent to which i can forgive you.
you. and all your well-made points

*Breeze Rustling Through Fall Flowers,* 1968. Acrylic on canvas, 57 ⅞ × 50 in. Phillips Collection, Washington, DC, Gift of Franz Bader.

so lemonade raised high and shivered back
and pocket candy swimming in your purse
my favorite color is you coming back
continual. the ocean is your hearse.

the fire is your apricot the bullet is your peach
the rolling hills of memory            your breach
i teach myself to keep you in a heart-shaped place
forever out of reach

and then forget

# savior index

my deepest grape is wine
my carbonated blood
becoming sky becoming earth becoming sun
and if all my breath is given
drowned by the river
dried by the shoreline
forget my name

and yet
that thin gold pathway
tennis bracelet way to heaven
godmother's favorite sweater
margarine jelly treat
embroiders my dreams in leftover thread
and so i need you

phantom fanta can hold me
through my melancholy summers
fathom fantasy bottom 40 songs

mosquito sweet my blood be syrup
my trace be goblet ribbon early sun
sugar and sleep deprivation drip
my name to paper
life into your hands

someone understands
what i didn't say
landscapes it into
scrape skittle riddle day

*Tiptoe Through the Tulips,* 1969. Acrylic on canvas, 50 × 48 in. National Gallery of Art, Washington, DC, Corcoran Collection, Gift of Vincent Melzac.

and I give you the puzzle back
fruit from the tree
and I give you the puzzle back
peels on the ground

and I could dance away from you
into the empty crease of books
hide in all the loopholes in the words

but i give you the question back
what happens
i give you the sunrise back
who wakes
i give you the water back
who drinks it
i give you the green grass back
to take

and rows and rows of citrus grafting
broken yard of trucks
memory melt
and slush salvation

# hindsight

i thought of you as sand
broken so fine you could shape me
i thought of you as astringent
so cleansing it stings

who knew you were the river
rushing so fast the salmon broke their backs
the beavers nearly drowned building the world

yes i planted torches around you
lit them on fire
lemongrass and citronella

yes i sang you a repetitive line
until you sung it back to me
like the good blues women
we must be

apologies
to the small membrane of your years
combustible nutritious sweet

gratitude
to the lessons of your time
half-life treasure
still burnishing my lungs
with breath

*Wind Dancing with Spring Flowers,* 1969. Acrylic on canvas, 50 5/16 × 48 1/16 in. Hood Museum of Art, Dartmouth College, Hanover, NH.

# afterlife index

the life where i jumped and you caught me
the life where we danced to mixtapes you made
the life where you bought me custom sneakers
the life where you paid for my beads and my braids
the life where i knew your eyes were oceans
the life where i thought your hands were trees
the life where i took your eternity for granted
i thought you would never leave

and when you did
my gut ripped itself out
i threw up all night
i suffered
because i thought this was the only life we had

but now i remember
the life where i was just some fugitive dancer
and you were just some warrior free
and i brought the spirit down into the fire
and you decided to die for me

and there are other lives i don't remember

show them all to me.

*Fiery Sunset,* 1973. Acrylic on canvas, 41 ¼ × 41 ¼ in. Museum of Modern Art, New York.

# palindrome before school

if play is prayer
then brushing my hair
into those bubble hairties and plastic barrettes
is like sweeping water onto shore
kneeling in the wet grass of morning
hoping to stand up clean
i mean my scalp holds ropes to cross the sea
adorned in fuchsia, purple, blue
wrapped up in grandma, nana, you
and in the first golden hour
when the sun reaches the forehead
of your salted mermaid child
you can imagine love is lavender, sea glass, pink
instead of vitamins, orange juice, eggs
you could feed me high tide, sunrise, gold
sunshade eyes hide tide to feed me
you could choose edge fight minds instead
and child of maids made from assault
your forehead teaches sunday school
your stolen shower
first in sand
you nan you mine you grand
you grand all wrapped in blue
per pull for sure and i adore
your cross i see your hopes
so mean and scalding clean
upstanding dream
and mourning class
keeling and short

*Untitled*, c. 1968. Watercolor on paper, 7 ¼ × 12 ⅛ in. Columbus Museum, GA, Gift of Miss John Maurice Thomas in memory of her parents, John H. and Amelia W. Cantey Thomas, and her sister Alma Woodsey Thomas.

on water
sleeping daughter
stop playing girl
let me fix
your crown

# seagrape

the exam booklet is her own sky
not a ceiling
not a ceiling

pencil her own diamond mine
don't trust her

is a beach vacation a receding carrot?

i don't know. fill my mouth with jewels
tell me that the fish tank is a skylight
i'll believe you

as much as i believe that sand is time
as much as i believe that love is blue
as much as i believe that what you know
can't ever be taken from you

i want to drink the paintbrush water
then i want to pee the sea
then i need a little daughter
at least as brown as me

before i become landscape
before i become song
before i become solar dust

*Air View of a Spring Nursery,* 1966. Acrylic on canvas, 48 × 48 in. Columbus Museum, GA, museum purchase and gift of the National Association of Negro Business Women, and the artist.

let me put my lipstick on
let me wear some nonsense shoes
cheer for all the wrong teams
skin my precious elbows
awkward knees

if you were a wayward seagrape
how would you divine
up and down through crabholes
sturdy midday shine

if you were a ready orange
heirloom grown by force
who would love your stems
who would follow your course

air and sky?
rain and snow?
evergreen trees you've never seen?
how would you know?

if the test is the ocean
the species fails
the underpaid teachers
are the whales

i'm just a seagrape
making soft from all this grit
sweet from the sureness of salt.

# salt account

watercolor is thick enough
when i wake with first blood
trained only by beverly cleary, judy blume
and a turquoise book with a big red dot
i wash my words with what i cannot see
watercolor is thick enough for me

ink is a drink
wasted on the satisfied
handwriting fails
i need a new notation
if i blot my ink in your open mouth
have the decent nerve to be thirsty

if i was a chemist i would keep vats of my blood
buckets of my sweat
ice trays of my tears

and mix them each time carefully
to make the different years

but i am not a chemist, nor a cleaner nor clear
only red
and black
and here

*Untitled,* early 1960s. Watercolor on paper, 22 × 30 in. Columbus Museum, GA, Gift of Miss John Maurice Thomas in memory of her parents, John H. and Amelia W. Cantey Thomas.

# disposable camera

*for Ayana, Laurie May, Mary Lauren, and Soraya*

in the time when all the lipstick
was named for bruises
i was eating skittles

in the age of grunge
i was embarrassingly bright
i started to wear black and white
in penance

when the depth of being
the only brown girls
kept us tight
we haunted bathrooms
during elective block
made up extra track practices
on days of good weather
just to stay after school together

i thought it was cool
how our different island mothers
terrified us in exactly the same way
their fear for us a language a lanyard a braid

and if we could have made freedom
out of soda bubbles
bricolage of plastic and jelly beans at the mall
we would have been so caddisfly and safe
in the bayside heat

*Snoopy Sees a Sunrise,* 1970. Acrylic on canvas, 48 × 48 in. National Air and Space Museum, Washington, DC.

i loved living with you
in a music video we were making up
grabbing the phone when they played our songs
three-way calling bored jewish boys all night long

BET had entirely too much space in our imaginations
our avatars ananda and amel larrieux
our gods 3T and immature

whatever are cul-de-sac girls to do
our eyes are brown
our lips are berry blue

# index instead of a drinking game

the teacher said use pencil
but the spirit said use blood
great grandpa said use earth
great grandma said yes mud
the aunties used their lipstick
and the uncles dealt in sludge
neighbors offered pepto-bismol
playmates gave me hugs
the priestess made a smoothie
our butches built a sturdy home
the ghosts brought georgia red clay
dad kept edison slate stone
mama gave her sticky insides
nana made a strong rum punch
passing strangers said try wheat grass
roommates traded orange crush
they offered everything they had
it's here
now cough it up

*Untitled* (study for *Red Nursery #4*), c. 1966. Acrylic on paper, 9 × 35 ½ in. David C. Driskell Center at the University of Maryland, College Park.

# packing list for the children

bring the blood on frozen ground
bring the blues that bruised you
bring the sun that dried you out
bring the breeze that used you
bring the laughter falling down
bring the sky that crashed
bring the mess you made before
bring your medicinal past
bring the smudged and clean again
bring the lemon flag
bring the pieces that you pieced
find a bigger bag
make the pieces peace again
wear your finest drag.

*Untitled,* 1968. Acrylic on cut, stapled, and taped paper, 18 ½ × 34 in. Steve and Lesley Testan Collection.

# impact report

this is what i did to my knees.

i trusted them.
i trusted them more than the pavement.

this is what i did to my skin.

i outgrew it.

this is what i did to my hands.

i reached for a sky that became the ground.

this is what i did to my wrist.

i let it break.

*

this is what my knees taught me.

ruby red jewels inside you.

this is what my skin taught me.

grow back.

this is what my hands told me.

it's not you that holds you up.

this is what my wrist whispered.

fly.

*Red Abstraction,* 1960. Oil on canvas, 36 ¼ × 30 in. David C. Driskell Center at the University of Maryland, College Park.

# from the ancestral chorus (come home when you want)

we send you forth
with tiny pieces of paper
                                        you will call them your teeth
we send you with tightly curled scrolls
                                        you will learn them as bones too

the first truth we told you

you will swim across many waters
                                        you call them days
arrive at many shorelines
                                        every night

you dream yourself

a breathing island
                                        we offer rest

twists and guidance
                                        everywhere you look
we say                                  we love we love we love you

    that's your name

*Babbling Brook and Whistling Poplar Trees Symphony,* 1976. Acrylic on canvas, 72 × 52 in. Michael Rosenfeld Gallery, New York.

# ekphrast

the swimming pool of your hands
the stem of your time      liming
the fruits of your ocean
all names for my love

the skin of your heart
colonnades of your breathing
sprite of your spirit
who you are who you are to me

tiny bricks of your blood cells
vast gasp of each lung
the shadow of you underneath
every heartbeat

a love poem
for you needs all the crimped thread
of the friendship bracelets i made
and disentangled

a love poem for you
needs every tone i learned
in school or at piano or at dance class
then forgot

a poem for you
is a road a home a waterway
a burning taste
a sacrificial snapshot

my love for you
so close to name and color
i would write it i would paint it
i cannot

*The Eagle Has Landed,* 1970–71. Acrylic on canvas, 50 ¼ × 50 ⅛ in. Private collection.

# alexis's prayer

rose petals
for the girl
who had to carry everything
sprinkle them on her heart

hibiscus for the child
who represented us all
may she release
all the water she held

zinnia confetti
for the free mind
of this child just now safe enough
to know herself as celebration

cinnamon carnation
for the breathing child
whose words meant too much

exhale

azaleas
may they easter from her chest
soft as dreams

azaleas
may they escape on the wind
where her hands cannot crush them

azaleas
may they kiss air
land gently on the waiting cheek
of everyone she could have been

*Red Azaleas Singing and Dancing to Rock and Roll Music,* 1976. Acrylic on three canvases, 73 ¾ × 158 ½ in. Smithsonian American Art Museum, Washington, DC.

# coda and acknowledgment

Primary is primary. First is first. The first thing I did every day for 365 days was to write down whatever arrived when I engaged Alma Thomas's paintings and photos from her archives. I learned so much about my own relationship to color. My associations. My longings. Sometimes every brushstroke took me into a different childhood memory. Sometimes I went to the bottom of the ocean and breathed my way back up. Sometimes I left the planet just to see it better. Sometimes I had a question for Alma. Sometimes I had questions for myself. Sometimes I felt like I was getting a message. Sometimes I just sat with the silence.

But always, the first person to hear any of the poems I considered worthy of air was Sangodare, also known as favorite child of the lightning, also known as the great love of my life. This is no accident. I have arranged my whole life to be a primary witness to and to be primarily witnessed by Sangodare.

It was Sangodare, inventor of a geological form of drawing that refracts words and faces into crystalline emergence, who was quite literally next to me as I walked through the Alma Thomas *Everything Is Beautiful* retrospective at the Frist in Nashville with my mouth hanging open. But the accompaniment goes much further than that. It is Sangodare who, when I mention offhand that I wrote about a butterfly, buys me three insect guidebooks and uses tracing papers to draw me my own window art of a butterfly native to Anguilla, one of my ancestral homelands. Which means, when I decided to live with the work of Alma Thomas as a daily practice for 365 days, I was already living with an artist. I was already involved in the collaborative art project of creating a life. Thank you, Sangodare, for giving me daily proof of beauty in this world.

And like Alma Thomas I take my status as an oldest sister very seriously. It is a primary identity. A factor in all my life decisions. I strive to live as a freedom exemplar for my sister, Ariana, and my brothers, Jared and Seneca. I have sought to live in a way that would open a way for you, first in your own imaginations. I want always to remind you of how much joy waits for you around every corner. Now all of my younger siblings are brilliant adults, living inspiring lives on your own terms. It is an understatement to say that I am a better person because of each of you than I ever could have been without you.

My mother, Pauline McKenzie, like Alma Thomas's mother, Amelia, spoke to me while I was still in her womb. My father, Clyde Gumbs, offered me his dreams. I am blessed to have parents who celebrated, emulated, and always supported the creativity coming through me.

I believe Alma Thomas was right to keep ever in mind the youngest among us. The artists all around us in the beauty of their possibility. My daily conversations with my nieces, the artists McKenzie and Penelope, offer me a bright world full of color. I feel like I'm flying.

Gratitude also to editor Jessie Kindig for championing this work. Thank you Ash Lago for your editorial support. Thank you to everyone at Yale University Press for your attention and care with this work. Thank you Jacqueline Goldsby for timely and helpful advice. Thank you Jonathan Frederick Walz for your enthusiasm and collaborative spirit and stewardship of Alma Thomas's legacy, and especially for including and contextualizing Alma Thomas's puppet work.

# sweetgeorgia

i loved you in layers while i became tree.
  i thickened myself with your heat.
i watch you with eyes colored by every day.

my brown is enough. is enough.

Cover of *Alma W. Thomas: A Retrospective Exhibition (1959–1966)*, April 24–May 17, 1966. Gallery of Art, College of Fine Arts, Howard University, Washington, DC. The image on the cover is mistitled "Resurrection."

# Notes

1. See Ida B. Wells.

2. Alma Thomas, "Artist's Statement" for the exhibition *Earth and Space Paintings,* Franz Bader Gallery, 1970.

3. H. E. Mahal, "Interviews: Four Afro-American Artists—Approaches to Inhumanity," *Art Gallery* 13, no. 7 (April 1970): 36. The phrase "man's inhumanity to man" is from the poem "Man Was Made to Mourn" by Scottish poet Robert Burns, first published in 1784.

4. Alma Thomas quoted in Regenia A. Perry, *Free Within Ourselves: African American Artists in the Collection of the National Museum of American Art* (National Museum of American Art, 1991), 170.

5. Gratitude to Christina Sharpe for "Beauty Is a Method," *e-flux,* no. 105 (December 2019), https://www.e-flux.com/journal/105/303916/beauty-is-a-method.

6. Richard A. Powell, "Colorstruck! Painting, Pigment, Affect," part 3, A. W. Mellon Lectures in the Fine Arts, National Gallery of Art, June 1, 2022, YouTube, 44:20, https://www.youtube.com/watch?v=E82WkYc6y6I&t=3337s.

7. Powell, "Colorstruck!," 4:33.

8. Powell, "Colorstruck!," 44:50.

9. Powell, "Colorstruck!," 45:10.

10. Kellie Jones, "To the Max: Energy and Experimentation," in *EyeMinded: Living and Writing Contemporary Art* (Duke University Press, 2011), 366.

11. Jones, "To the Max," 379.

12. For more on the materials for the *Pass Carry Hold* exhibition by the Residency Program at the Studio Museum of Harlem, see "Micro/Macro," *Studio Magazine,* December 5, 2024, https://www.studiomuseum.org/magazine/micro-macro.

13. Robin Wall Kimmerer, *Braiding Sweetgrass: Indigenous Wisdom, Scientific Knowledge and the Teachings of Plants* (Milkweed, 2013), 132.

14. Sofia Samatar quoted in Ashon Crawley, *The Lonely Letters* (Duke University Press, 2020), 49.

15. Jacob Kainen, "Alma W. Thomas: Order and Emotion," in *Alma Thomas: A Retrospective of the Paintings,* by Sachi Yarari et al. (Pomegranate, 1998), 37.

16. Powell, "Colorstruck!," 45:10.

17. Powell, "Colorstruck!," 45:30.

18. Powell, "Colorstruck!," 45:45.

19. Powell, "Colorstruck!," 46:10.

20. Powell, "Colorstruck!," 3:10.

21. Powell, "Colorstruck!," 3:10.

22. Powell, "Colorstruck!," 3:10.

23. bell hooks, "The Poetics of Soul: Art for Everyone," in *Art on My Mind: Visual Politics* (W. W. Norton, 1995), 21.

24. Jonathan P. Binstock, "Apolitical Art in a Political World: Alma Thomas in the Late 1960s and Early 1970s," in Yarari et al., *Retrospective of the Paintings,* 54.

25. bell hooks, "Introduction," in *Art on My Mind,* xi. Emphasis mine.

26. Faith Ringgold, "The 1960s: Is There a Black Art?," in *We Flew over the Bridge: The Memoirs of Faith Ringgold* (Duke University Press, 2005), 147.

27. Mahal, "Interviews," 36.

28. Jones, "To the Max," 379.

29. Faith Ringgold, "Teaching Art: Those Who Can Should," in *We Flew over the Bridge,* 230.

30. Lou Stovall quoted in Ann Gibson, "Putting Alma Thomas in Place: Modernist Painting, Color Theory and Civil Rights," in Yarari et al., *Retrospective of the Paintings,* 38–39.

31. Alma Thomas quoted in Kainen, "Order and Emotion," 33.

32. hooks, "Introduction," xi.

33. June Jordan, "The Creative Spirit: Children's Literature," in *Revolutionary Mothering: Love on the Frontlines,* ed. Alexis Pauline Gumbs, China Martens, and Mai'a Williams (PM Press, 2014), 11.

34. See Rebecca Bush, "Sand Unshaken: The Origins Story of Alma Thomas," in *Alma Thomas: Everything Is Beautiful,* ed. Seth Feman and Jonathan Frederick Walz (Yale University Press, 2021), 27–42.

35. Ntozake Shange with Aidan Flax Clark, host, in *Library Talks,* podcast, "Ntozake Shange on Inspiration and Harlem," February 6, 2015, https://podcasts.apple.com/us/podcast/ntozake-shange-on-inspiration-harlem/id804982781?i=1000334978362.

36. Ntozake Shange, "A Note to the Reader," in *Ridin' the Moon in Texas: Word Paintings* (St. Martin's Press, 1987), xi.

37. Evie Shockley quoted in National Book Foundation, "Author Bio: Evie Shockley," https://www.nationalbook.org/people/evie-shockley/.

38. Evie Shockley, "Where and When 'I' Enters," "Why Me? Colloquium on First Person Writing in the Age of Fictionalized Fact," Cogut Institute for the Humanities, Brown University, May 9, 2024, YouTube, https://www.youtube.com/watch?v=ZuVwULSB6oY.

39. Evie Shockley, "alma's arkestral vision (or farther out)," in *Suddenly We* (Wesleyan University Press, 2023), 9. ©2023 by Evie Shockley. Published by Wesleyan University Press. Used with Permission.

40. Kevin Quashie, *Black Aliveness, or a Poetics of Being* (Duke University Press, 2021), 154.

41. Quashie, *Black Aliveness*, 154.

42. *Alma Thomas: Everything Is Beautiful*, a retrospective at the Frist Museum of Art in Nashville, February 25–June 22, 2022. Also see The Art Story, "Alma Thomas," https://www.theartstory.org/artist/thomas-alma.

43. Steve Abrams, "Tony Sarg," in *World Encyclopedia of Puppetry Arts*, 2012, https://wepa.unima.org/en/tony-sarg/.

44. Diploma signed by Alma Thomas, from Tony Sarg's summer puppetry course, in Jonathan Fredrick Walz, "Alma Thomas: 'The Marionette Show as a Correlating Activity in Public Schools,' " in *Living Objects: African American Puppetry Essays* (Ballard Institute and Museum of Puppetry, 2019), 6.

45. Alma W. Thomas, "The Marionette Show as a Correlating Activity in the Public Schools" (MA thesis, Columbia University, 1934).

46. Mahal, "Interviews," 36. The phrase "man's inhumanity to man" is from the poem "Man Was Made to Mourn" by Scottish poet Robert Burns, first published in 1784.

47. John Maurice Thomas, oral history transcript, 1986, Alma Thomas Papers, c. 1894–2001, box 1, folder 28, page 20, Archives of American Art, Smithsonian Institution, Washington, DC.

48. Alma Thomas quoted in Smithsonian American Art Museum, "Red Azaleas Singing and Dancing to Rock and Roll Music," https://americanart.si.edu/artwork/red-azaleas-singing-and-dancing-rock-and-roll-music-24017.

49. Feman and Walz, *Everything Is Beautiful*, 254.

50. Alma Thomas quoted in Smithsonian American Art Museum, "Red Azaleas Singing."

51. Grace Lee Boggs, "Revolutionaries, Evolutionaries, Solutionaries," [R]evolution: James and Grace Lee Boggs Center, https://www.boggscenter.org/writings/revolutionaries-evolutionaries-solutionaries.

52. Surah Luqman 31:29.

53. Adrian Piper, "On Conceptual Art," in *Out of Order, Out of Sight*, vol. 1, *Selected Writings in Meta-Art, 1968–1992* (MIT Press, 1996), 241. The epigraphs in this essay are from Adrian Piper, "Xenophobia and the Indexical Present I: Essay," in *Out of Order*, 245, 248.

54. Powell, "Colorstruck!," 3:10.

55. Piper, "Xenophobia," 257.

56. Adrian Piper, "Flying," in *Out of Order*, 223.

57. Piper, "Flying," 224.

58. Piper, "Xenophobia," 247–48.

59. Piper, "Xenophobia," 257.

60. Alma Thomas quoted in Gibson, "Putting Alma Thomas in Place," 41.

61. Piper, "Xenophobia," 248.

62. Jamaica Kincaid, *See Now Then* book event, Seattle Public Library, May 2, 2019.

63. M. Jacqui Alexander, *Pedagogies of Crossing: Meditations on Feminism, Sexual Politics, Memory, and the Sacred* (Duke University Press, 2004), 246.

64. Alexander, *Pedagogies of Crossing*, 246.

65. Kincaid, *See Now Then* book event.

66. Kincaid, *See Now Then* book event.

67. Kincaid, *See Now Then* book event.

68. Jamaica Kincaid, *See Now Then* (Farrar Straus and Giroux, 2013), 14–16.

69. Kincaid, *See Now Then,* 142.

70. Kincaid, *See Now Then,* 143.

71. Alexander, *Pedagogies of Crossing,* 246.

72. Alexander, *Pedagogies of Crossing,* 254.

73. Audre Lorde, "Call," in *The Collected Poems of Audre Lorde* (W. W. Norton, 1997), 599.